FREEING SOMEONE YOU LOVE

—*from*—

EATING DISORDERS

Mary Dan Eades, M. D.

THE BODY PRESS/PERIGEE
Produced by the Philip Lief Group, Inc.

for my grandmother, Kathleen Dillon,
with love, admiration, and deep appreciation

This book concerns identifying and helping persons who suffer from eating disorders. It is intended as a general guide and not as a replacement for medical advice. Final decisions about treatment must be made by each individual in consultation with his or her physician and family. The publisher and the author expressly disclaim liability for adverse consequences resulting from the implementation of suggestions contained in this book.

Perigee Books
are published by
The Putnam Publishing Group
200 Madison Avenue
New York, NY 10016
Produced by The Philip Lief Group, Inc.
6 West 20th Street New York, NY 10011
Copyright © 1993 by Mary Dan Eades, M.D., and
The Philip Lief Group, Inc.

Library of Congress Cataloging-in-Publication Data

Eades, Mary Dan.
Freeing someone you love from eating disorders / Mary Dan Eades.
p.   cm.
Includes bibliographical references and index.
ISBN 0-399-51782-0
1. Eating disorders.   2. Eating disorders—Treatment.   3. Eating
disorders—Patients—Rehabilitation.   I. Title.
RC552.E18E24   1993
616.85'26—dc20   92-30799   CIP

Printed in the United States of America

1 2 3 4 5 6 7 8 9 10

This book is printed on acid-free paper.

∞

Acknowledgments

I wish to thank, first and foremost, my family for putting up with my very erratic moods during the turbulent production of this book, especially my husband, best friend, and confidant, Mike: I couldn't have finished it without having you to "spot" for me. And thanks to Scott, Dan, and Ted, my boys, for cutting me some slack when I needed it.

Thanks to the helpful and friendly people at AA/BA in New York, to Marilyn Means at Pinnacle Point Hospital in Little Rock, and to Teri Haskins and Larry Cole for taking time out to give me their professional input.

Contents

Introduction   7

1: Anatomy of an Eating Disorder   11

2: The Making of a Disordered Eater   33

3: Look, Listen, and Feel—How to Recognize an Eating
   Disorder   55

4: Helping Your Loved One Help Herself   72

5: Twelve Steps to Your Own Freedom   110

6: Current Therapies for Disordered Eating   123

7: Healing the Home   150

Notes   173

Resources for Help   176

Suggested Readings   177

Bibliography   180

Stressor Worksheet   182

Index   185

Introduction

When I decided to write this book, I did so with the hope of offering help and support to the many people out there who suffer the emotional anguish of watching a loved one tortured by an eating disorder. Because you are reading it, you must know such a person or think that you do. And so it is you to whom I reach out. To you, who want so desperately to help your daughters* or wives or friends, but don't know how. I hope to tell you how; I hope to give you the understanding and direction you lack. Toward that end, I have included information and guidelines that will assist you in determining whether or not your loved one does suffer from an eating disorder, information that will improve your understanding of the illnesses and will underscore the fact that the eating disorder itself is but a symptom of a deeper and more important problem, a signal flag, if you will, that there is emotional work to be done. Most important, I hope to offer you a direction, to set you on the road that leads in a stepwise fashion toward freedom, that helps point you to various resources where you will perhaps find solutions for you and your loved one who is suffering.

Although I have never suffered from compulsive overeating, been anorectic or bulimic, nor has anyone in my family, I have

---

* Throughout this book I will use female pronouns to refer to sufferers of eating disorders, because these problems occur far and away more frequently in women than in men. I have done this to streamline the writing and not to imply that the disorders do not occur in men as well. They do, and with just as much devastation to the male sufferer and his family as to the female.

seen at close range the havoc these illnesses wreak upon the young women in their grip and upon those who love them. I have seen it because I have been a physician in general practice for over a decade, and the increasing incidence of these disorders alone would have put me in proximity with them: with 1 in 250 young women (and in some age categories 1 in 100) potentially subject to aberrant eating behavior, a busy general practitioner could hardly escape running into a number of affected patients. Although startlingly fewer cases of the eating disorders occur in men than women—bulimia, for example, occurs nearly 45 times more commonly in young women by college age—the disorders are not exclusive to the female gender. In my clinical practice, a part of our focus is on nutrition and metabolic control of obesity and related problems. That focus has brought to our doors disordered eaters of all three major types, but especially of compulsive overeaters. And yet, beyond the scope of a single practitioner's private practice, there are many more people in need of this information that a book on the disorders could reach, and it is to these suffering families I wish to offer my help and expertise.

To broaden my clinical experience, and in preparation for writing, I began reading much of the current medical literature, recent research, and lay literature, and this exercise brought a few surprises. As a general practitioner, while I do not generally undertake psychotherapy for disordered eating, I have diagnosed the behaviors in my patients, I have helped them find appropriate therapy, and I have taken care of the physical ills that befall them because of their compulsions. I felt I had a pretty clear understanding of them, and in general, I did. However, a thorough reading of the newest literature—especially on the neurobiological frontiers—reminded me once again how quickly medical certainty and understanding can change. These new frontiers of research will change the face of what physicians have been taught to believe about these disorders. Whatever I might have thought of as "fact" beforehand, the work now coming out of the research circles changed even my understanding of the inner workings of these disorders and heightened my index of suspicion for spotting disordered eating behavior among my patients. I had thought I understood, but as is so often the case as current thinking gives way to newer ideas, perhaps I had not. With this realization, it dawned on me that certainly I was not alone in my need to revamp some of the tenets I had relied on. There are likely many other physicians and health care professionals who also labor under the delusion that they *know* when they do not. And so, in a sense, I speak to them as well. I hope that by reading, they, too, will raise their consciousness about the disorders and become more aware of the subtle clues their anorectic, bulimic, or compulsively overeating patients are surely passing to them. If their reading this book causes them to pick up on these clues and their increased awareness helps even one young woman to admit to and confront her behavior, their time will have been well spent. And so will mine.

Writing this book has been an odyssey for me, a journey out of my own set beliefs about disordered eating and into the light of a newer and better understanding. Join me now, and together we'll debunk the myths about these behaviors; we'll explore them, dissect them, and subject them to the bright light of scientific inquiry, and from that study, discover what kinds of forces drive the disordered eater's psyche to pursue so self-destructive a path against all logic or reason. Come with me and learn how you can help to free someone you love from an eating disorder.

Chapter One

Anatomy of an Eating Disorder

The crash awoke Bill from a dead sleep. It sounded as if an army of burglars had broken down the front door of the apartment. He reached over to the other side of the bed where his wife Ellen should also have been jolted awake, but his hand encountered only cold bedsheets. Where on earth could she be at this hour? Who was in the house? Bill threw back the covers and bolted into the hallway, heading in the direction of the sound. From the crack around the kitchen door, light spilled into the hall, and he inched his way along the corridor, trying not to alert whoever had made the noise, until he came even with the door. He could hear them, still in there, but less noisy now, trying to be quiet. Where was Ellen? He called out her name in a hoarse whisper, and the kitchen noises fell silent. They'd heard him. No time now to play coy. No time to look for Ellen. He burst through the door and came face-to-face not with burglars, but with his wife, sitting cross-legged in front of the refrigerator spreading peanut butter and mayonnaise onto a cupcake and stuffing it into her mouth. Around her, broken jars and bottles spilled globs of jelly and pickles and mustard onto the floor where they had landed. The bottom shelf of the refrigerator door hung by one end. At first he couldn't put it all together. Obviously the shelf had fallen and spilled all its contents—the giant crash that had awakened him—but why was Ellen just sitting in the middle of it eating? Why had she made no motion to clean it up? That wasn't like her. Why was she looking at him now so strangely, as though he'd done something wrong? He couldn't utter a single word when she pushed past him, headed for the bathroom, and slammed the door behind her.

Bill and Ellen* had met in graduate school. Both were excellent students, hardworking, exacting. After graduation, four years ago, they had married and settled into the perfect "yuppie" life: two fast-track careers, two cars, great condo in the city, and a small vacation place on the water. They worked long hours but had agreed that until their careers and financial base were secure, job duties came first. And that usually meant catching moments together when they could find them. Nothing in their relationship to this point had prepared him for what he had just seen. Stunned and confused, Bill retrieved the dustpan and mop from the utility closet and began to pick up the mess. From the bathroom, he could hear Ellen vomiting. Although he didn't really understand it at this point, Bill thought he had at least an inkling now of what was going on. Ellen had anorexia or bulimia, one of those eating problems. He'd heard of women with these problems; hadn't everyone in this day and age? But he never dreamed his Ellen was one of them.

But Bill's concerns are well-founded; Ellen's behavior is indeed bulimic. She may be one of the 10,000 or more young women diagnosed this year[1] with an abnormal eating behavior that drives them to stuff themselves with huge quantities of food—sometimes 10,000 or more calories in a few hours—and then force themselves to vomit all or most of it back up. Sometimes they repeat this cycle three, four, five, even more times each day. Why? Why do these people, like Ellen, engage in what appears at least on the surface to be a voluntary behavior that not only seems bizarre to most of us, but is destructive? And who are these 10,000 Americans who succumb to bulimia each year? What, if

* The people fictionalized for the case histories used in the scenarios for this book serve as typical examples of patients or families struggling to understand and overcome the various eating disorders. Any resemblance to any person living or dead is coincidental.

any, characteristics do they share? More important to those of you who have such concerns about someone you love, how can you—as friend, spouse, or relative—know when or even whether to worry and what to do? I will address each of these concerns as we progress, but for now, let's get acquainted with the enemy itself; let's put a face to these eating disorders. First we'll look at the who, the what, and the when for each of the eating disorders. Then we'll turn our attention to the why, examining the psychological disruption that usually underlies disordered eating. I want to begin by examining bulimia nervosa to see if we can piece together characteristics that will bring a picture of the "typical" bulimic into clearer focus.

Vital Statistics: The Profile of Bulimia Nervosa

• **The bulimic is usually female.** As with the related and perhaps more widely known condition of anorexia nervosa, which we will profile in a moment, a dramatic gender gap exists in bulimia: women account for the vast majority of cases, with men making up a mere 5 to 10 percent. Some studies estimate that as many as 18 percent of young women (and only 0.4 percent of young men) have engaged in bulimic behavior by freshman year of college. While puberty seems to be the stress point for the onset of bulimia for women, it holds no such agonies for young men in our society. In fact, quite the reverse is true. Young men at puberty not only strive to beef up, but receive encouragement from parents, coaches, and friends to "Eat up!" For adolescent males, putting on pounds equates with vitality, desirability, and athletic prowess. The typical comment as adolescent boys pile their plates and increase their size runs something like, "My, you're growing up to be such a big fine man!" Quite a different spin on weight than that for young girls. Cultural molding, then, at least in part may explain the enormous gender disparity for this disorder.

• **The bulimic is usually white.** Although the disorder cuts across all racial lines, again, as with anorexia, the overwhelming preponderance of cases occur among Caucasians. However, the validity of this apparent racial disparity is perhaps questionable, because the differences may be more reflective of the disorder's strong association to affluence than to some as-yet-undetermined genetic predisposition that afflicts members of one race more than another. Mountains of new research into a possible organic cause—most notably research into abnormalities in the release and use of certain brain chemicals—may yet prove a genetic predisposition that would explain the racial (or even gender) disparities. I'll delve more deeply into this aspect in a later section, but for now let's move on.

• *The bulimic behavior most often begins in the teen years,* but may carry on for a decade or more, often going unsuspected by family or friends for many years. The onset of the disorder frequently occurs during or just after the puberty growth spurt in the early teen years. As young women progress through puberty, the stimulation of the female reproductive hormones signals the laying down of a modest increase in body fat and a natural sculpting of what will become a mature female shape. The extra padding associated with this expansion of hips and breasts (in this society where svelte high-fashion models are projected as the norm) may cause developing young women to despair that obesity is surely around the corner for them. For most adolescents and teens, fat is out and thin is in. In reality, it's probably unfair to limit that particular maxim to such a young age group; in this nation, I fear, there is no age limit on the "thin is in" feeling, most especially for women. But all too often, this fat-o-phobia prompts girls at very early ages to begin dieting—or at least to become self-conscious about how much they weigh, how much they eat, what size they wear—and some of them carry the phobia to an extreme. In other words, early weight concerns may lead some of them to develop eating disorders.

Let me stress at this point that abnormal eating behavior is far more complex in its origin than calling it the simple product of media bombardment would suggest. Obviously, the overwhelming majority of young women in America receive the same advertising hype and fewer than one in five develop eating disorders.

Perhaps, then, the gotta-be-thin message must fall onto fertile emotional ground, with some young women naturally more at risk in this regard than others. The development of the disorders results from a complex interplay of the thin message superimposed on a background of psychological disruption, family dysfunction, and perhaps biological predisposition. We'll examine this more closely in the next chapter, which is devoted to the psychological underpinnings of these behaviors, but let's continue now to complete the general profile we've begun.

• **_The bulimic is more often socioeconomically affluent._** Some debate exists about why this should be. Are there specific forces, social pressures, or stresses among the more affluent families—such as a mind-set typified by the Duchess of Windsor's famous maxim: You can't be too rich or too thin!—that drive greater numbers of young women in this segment of our society toward bulimia? Or are the higher numbers of cases among affluent families the result of greater health awareness in this group or greater access to specialized medical care, making these young women more likely to seek care and thus more likely to be diagnosed as bulimic? Could it even be nothing more than a desire among affluent families for a trendy diagnosis, a "me, too" syndrome—i.e., yes, our daughter has bulimia, too? At this point, medical research has not given us a clear answer as to why this group seems riddled by cases of bulimia, but the question bears greater scrutiny, which it will surely receive as the case numbers continue to climb. What is not in doubt is a clear predilection for affluent young women to succumb to this abnormal eating behavior.

• **_The bulimic probably appears normal physically._** By that I mean that there is not usually any easy-to-spot outward sign that would tell us that a woman is bulimic. Although she will virtually always display a greater-than-normal concern for her weight (some bulimics can't pass a scale without getting on it or a mirror without checking it) and continually strive toward thinness, the bulimic may maintain a weight very close to normal for her height and thus may _appear_ to be of sound and normal health and stature. Underlying this outwardly normal facade, however, there may be many medical problems brewing, such as blood chemistry disturbances (usually potassium and sodium imbalances) that can lead to abnormal—serious or even fatal— heart rhythms, fainting spells, or muscle cramping. And the caustic effects of stomach acid from frequent vomiting can ulcerate and erode the lining of the esophagus (the tube that carries food between the mouth and stomach), can lead to chronic or persistent sore throats, and can destroy the enamel of the teeth. Persistent abrasions or calluses on the back of the hand or fingers (which occur when she forces herself to vomit) may offer subtle outward clues to hidden purging behavior. But to the casual eye, none of this would show. The world usually sees a "perfectly normal" person.

• *The bulimic often exercises compulsively.* It is not uncommon for family and friends of bulimic women (or men*) to view them as "health nuts" who exercise night and day and eat only the most Spartan diets: low in calories and low in fat, eschewing gooey desserts, munching on carrot sticks and sipping mineral water. And in our fitness-crazed society, who would not look upon such behavior with awe and admiration? That's what we're all supposed to be doing in theory, right? In basic principle, certainly a life of dietary discretion and healthy exercise would suit most of us better. But the bulimic individual's ultrarigorous regimen of diet and exercise is far from a striving toward some noble ideal; rather, it is usually an attempt to "repair" or "undo" the effects of their bingeing addiction. Compulsive exercise, for bulimics, becomes a purge substitute—burning away the caloric evidence of what bulimic men and women usually view as their awful secret. The bulimic abuses exercise as a "cure" instead of (or often in addition to) vomiting up the evidence or attempting to force evacuation of the evidence through abuse of laxatives, diuretics (water pills), or enemas.

---

* Although, as I have said, men comprise only a small percentage of cases of bulimia or anorexia, when they do, compulsive exercise is most often the "purge technique" of choice among men. It may take the form of running or weight training or even aerobic classes.

• *The bulimic usually views her disordered eating behavior as distinctly abnormal.* Bulimics *know* fully and completely that what they're doing is odd, and they usually have a strong sense of guilt or even personal loathing for continuing to do it, but they also feel powerless not to succumb. Most bulimics follow each binge and purge with a vow never to do it again, and many wake up each day pledging that today they will win out over their secret habit. Hiding the "terrible truth" about themselves from all the world, they live in desperate fear of discovery and a certainty that once the truth is known, they will be rejected. In fact, once discovered, bulimic individuals often actually experience a sense of relief that the secret is out and are generally more eager than their anorexic counterparts to work toward getting rid of their symptoms.

• *The bulimic individual is often impulsive in other ways as well.* And this impulsive character may lead her into addictive behaviors that go beyond food and exercise. Of the three major eating-disordered groups—anorexics, bulimics, and compulsive overeaters—the bulimic is the one most likely to have problems dealing with drugs, alcohol, or impromptu sex, with some figures placing the occurrence of alcohol or drug abuse in bulimics in the range of 15 to 25 percent.[2] This is not to imply that all bulimic women succumb to these other addictions, only that these behaviors—because they are also impulsive in nature—are more commonly seen in the bulimic group than the others.

Although each case is different, bulimics often share several basic characteristics that make up a general profile and represent the salient features of the disease. According to the *Diagnostic and Statistical Manual of Mental Disorders*, 3rd edition, revised[3] (or DSM-III-R as it is known), there are five criteria that must be present for a clinician (physician, psychologist, or social worker) to make the diagnosis of bulimia nervosa. These are:

1. Recurrent episodes of binge eating (rapid consumption of a large amount of food in a discrete period of time).
2. A feeling of lack of control over eating behavior during the eating binges.

3. The person regularly engages in either self-induced vomiting, use of laxatives or diuretics, strict dieting or fasting, or vigorous exercise in order to prevent weight gain.
4. A minimum average of two binge eating episodes a week for at least three months.
5. Persistent overconcern with body shape and weight.

From these general attributes, we can begin to formulate a picture of the bulimic. We'll return to this picture later and bring it into sharper focus when we begin to examine the psychological forces that may feed into or drive her abnormal behavior in a subsequent section, so keep these broad characteristics in mind. But for now, let's leave Ellen and Bill and bulimia and take a look at the case of a young woman who suffers from the next of the three major eating disorders, which is closely related to bulimia but much more widely known: anorexia nervosa.

Lindsey sat alone in her room, studying for tomorrow's history exam. In the circle of light at her desk, she pored over stacks of orderly index cards, reading and reciting the information written on them in her small, neat script. She had gotten perfect scores on all her exams in that class so far this term and didn't want to "mess up" at this point. Beside her on the window shelf sat her untouched dinner tray, the food on it congealed now from sitting for over an hour. She had allowed herself a bottle of mineral water as she studied, but she'd had a couple of grapes and three crackers at lunch, and that was really more than she'd wanted anyway. She didn't need the food, really, and certainly didn't want that huge plate of pork chops and dressing and vegetables that her mother had fixed. It made her stomach heave just to look at it, so she'd covered it with her napkin. But she couldn't say she didn't want it; her folks just wouldn't understand that she was in control, she was different. For the first time since she was described in high school as a "pudgy sophomore," she felt in control. She felt proud of how well she could manage her life and her weight. Sure, she still wasn't perfect, but at 103 pounds, she was closer.

"Lindsey! Have you finished your supper?" she could hear her mom calling as she climbed the stairs to her room.

"Yes, Mother." Lindsey snatched up the full plate, dumped its contents

into a trash bag beneath the desk—she'd ditch that later when everyone was asleep—and met her mother at the door with a smile and an empty dinner tray.

"Great dinner, thanks. Gotta keep studying. Big test tomorrow. Night, Mom." Lindsey pushed the tray into her mother's hands and closed the door.

Lindsey's mom, Rita, and her dad, Tom, had noticed Lindsey's weight dropping. She'd been just the merest tad on the plump side a year ago when she'd entered ninth grade, and when she'd begun to slim down a bit, Rita had been thrilled. She had fought a bit of a weight problem herself and was happy that maybe Lindsey wouldn't have to. But now, Rita thought, Lindsey seemed to be getting a little too thin in spite of an all-out effort to prepare tasty foods that would encourage her daughter to eat more. And although she cleaned her plate most nights, she didn't seem to be gaining any weight. At 5'5", she was downright wraithlike now.

Rita had attributed Lindsey's weight change to stress at school and late nights studying. Certainly, Lindsey seemed to be excelling there—top of her class in just about every subject. In fact, she was so wrapped up in school and schoolwork that she hardly ever took time out to sit down and eat with the family anymore. And on the rare occasions when she did, she seemed so distracted that she barely picked at her food. She would always excuse herself early to get back to her books, pleading that she was either not hungry right now or too keyed up over an upcoming exam to eat.

It was probably just a phase she was going through, Rita told herself, but if Lindsey got much thinner, she was taking her to the doctor. Something had to be wrong for her to continue losing so much weight.

Rita knows or at least senses that something is amiss with Lindsey, but it has not occurred to her at this point that the something is an eating disorder. She does not yet realize that her daughter is anorectic, because most anorexic young women cleverly cover the telltale tracks of their disorder—just as Lindsey scrapes the food into a bag and disposes of it later. Until the physical results of the fasting finally become obvious, oftentimes no one suspects a thing. And sadly, unless Lindsey wants to come forward with the truth about her behavior, even a visit to the doctor will probably not pinpoint the real problem at this stage.

In the early stages of anorexia, there is little physical evidence except the weight loss. The lack of symptoms early on is because although these young women do restrict their intake—albeit to sometimes startlingly low levels of calories, on the order of a minuscule 300 to 400 per day—they usually do not engage in regular purging tactics like their bulimic cousins. No vomiting, laxatives, diuretics, or enemas in this group, just shockingly little to eat, which they may disguise, as Lindsey did, by throwing food away or pretending to eat elsewhere. Please note that although at this point I am addressing these two disorders—bulimia and anorexia—as two separate and distinct entities, there is often a good deal of overlap. The two can coexist in an eating behavior termed *bulimarexia*, in which there are features of both disorders. For the sake of clarity, however, let's stick for now to the "pure" forms of these disorders and take a look at the profile of the typical anorectic.

Vital Statistics: The Profile of Anorexia Nervosa

• *The anorexic disorder, like bulimia, occurs almost exclusively in young girls and women,* in whites more than any other race, and in the socioeconomically affluent for all the same reasons cited previously for bulimics.

• *The anorexic behavior usually begins—although a little earlier than the bulimic behavior—in adolescence,* with the slight weight gain and redistribution of body fat that naturally occurs with the puberty growth spurt. The weight change triggers a desire to be thinner, which leads to modest (at first) attempts to diet and reduce. But in the anorexic personality—if such exists—the success and feeling of empowerment or control over weight and eating may not end with attaining a "normal" or "healthy" new weight. What begins innocently as modest reduction gradually evolves into a full-blown obsession with weight and diet. The anorectic will continue to feel fat, even at weights clearly below normal.

• ***The anorectic suffers from a major distortion of body image.*** Most of us have stepped in front of a fun-house mirror at a circus or a carnival and seen our shape stretch long and spidery or watched it grow squat and wide. Such a distortion of image is not unlike what happens in the mind of the anorectic. Even when starved down to a point where she is all angles—elbows, knees, ribs, and shoulder blades—the anorectic will insist she is still too fat, and no amount of talk can persuade her otherwise. She can plainly see that she is fat, so why can't you? She considers the distortion to be in *other people's* view and not in her own.

• ***The anorectic usually excels scholastically.*** These young women often achieve great success in their studies and even in their work. But they may succumb to the scholarly equivalent of compulsive exercising: compulsive studying. They may retire to their room or to the library and cloister themselves away with their books (a very socially acceptable behavior to adults) to avoid food confrontations.

• ***The anorectic is usually a pleaser.*** She's the "good girl," tending to be reliable, helpful, polite, and compliant in virtually every facet of her life *except in regard to her refusal to eat.* This act of rebellion may be her only one, but she will cling tenaciously to her rigid control over her weight and food intake.

• ***The anorectic will finally show very obvious physical signs of her disorder, chief among them extreme thinness,*** usually significantly below the normal weight for her height. The typical anorectic has a body mass index, or BMI, in the range of 16.[4] You can easily determine your own or your loved one's BMI by consulting the table on page 22.[5]

Other physical signs of malnourishment—dry skin, brittle hair and nails—finally become apparent. And like the bulimic, brewing beneath the surface bubbles a whole host of potential medical problems not visible to the casual glance, such as constipation, anemia, dehydration that can lead to fainting spells, blood chemistry imbalances that could stir up the same kind of abnormal heart rhythms as in bulimics, depression of the metabolic drive,

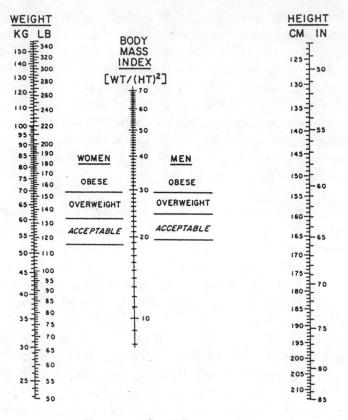

Nomogram for Body Mass Index.

and hormonal deficiencies. Low levels of the reproductive hormones brought about by malnutrition will ultimately lead to loss of normal menstrual cycles and, at least temporarily, infertility, which all anorexic women experience.

• ***Unlike the bulimic, the anorectic usually does not view her behavior as abnormal.*** She may tend, in fact, to feel a sense of self-righteous zeal about her refusal to eat. Even when faced with severe threats to her health or even to her life, the anorexic individual does not easily accept any treatment that might cause her to regain any weight. For example, the authors of a psychiatric text[6] describe the case of two anorectic patients admitted to the hospital to receive total parenteral nutrition (formulated food given by IV catheter) in an attempt to reverse their life-threatening starvation. In order to "save" themselves from the possibility of weight gain from the force feeding by vein, the patients actually emptied the nutritional liquid out of their IV bottles and refilled them with regular tap water. In doing so, they risked contracting severe—even potentially life-threatening—infection from contamination of the intravenous line, as well as the possibility of fatal air embolism, i.e., letting large air bubbles into the intravenous line during the change, the consequences of which can be brain damage or a stroke. Both patients recognized the risks, and both preferred taking their chances on these worst-case outcomes to the specter of gaining weight.

As we saw previously with bulimia (and as is the case for every psychiatric disorder), the experts recognize several key features of anorexia common to all patients with the disorder. By the book—that text being the aforementioned DSM-III-R—psychiatrists rule that the four criteria that must be present to make the diagnosis of anorexia nervosa are:

1. Refusal to maintain body weight over a minimal normal weight for age and height—e.g., weight loss leading to maintenance of body weight 15 percent below that expected; or failure to make expected weight gain during period of growth, leading to body weight 15 percent below that expected.
2. Intense fear of gaining weight or becoming fat, even though underweight.
3. Disturbance in the way in which one's body weight, size, or shape is experienced—e.g., the person claims to "feel fat" even when emaciated, believes that one area of the body is "too fat" even when obviously underweight.
4. In females, absence of at least three consecutive menstrual cycles when otherwise expected to occur (primary or secondary amenorrhea).

We'll explore the psychosocial theories about what underlies the anorectic's behavior a bit later. For now let's begin roughly sketching in the broad shapes of this disorder. Then, as you progress through the text, expanding your understanding of anorexia, we will add more detail. What of the third disorder? Compulsive overeating? Let's look at an example.

The driver behind Susan honked loudly, and she jerked her head up to see the car in front already far ahead. She hadn't noticed that the light had turned green, because she'd been struggling to open the box of powdered-sugar donuts on the seat beside her. She'd demolished the first box of a dozen between the store and here, and although the anxious feeling in the pit of her stomach had diminished, it hadn't gone away. She stuffed another bite of donut into her mouth with a sigh of resignation.

"Why did you even put your name in for the promotion?" she said aloud to herself as she drove. "You should have known it would go to Jill, you idiot." It always does, she thought. Always to the skinny, pretty, shiny-haired, tan ones with cute names like Jill. They get all the breaks. She shoved the rest of the donut into her mouth and picked up another. By the time she pulled into the driveway and parked next to her husband's pickup, nothing remained of two dozen donuts but a dusting of powdered sugar on the bottoms of the boxes, but she didn't feel so down. She buried the empty containers beneath the trash in the can beside the door so George wouldn't see them and gingerly brushed away any telltale crumbs from her lips with her fingers.

"Honey, I'm home," she called out as she opened the door.

"Well, how'd it go today at work?" George said.

"Fine. Just fine. But I'm too bushed to cook tonight. Why don't we go out to that new Mexican place that opened last week? I've been dying to try it out."

"Why not. Do we have something to celebrate? Did you get the promotion?"

"Uh-uh. No, but it's all right. I mean, I'm okay about it and all. You know, when I think about it, it's probably just as well, because I would have had to change offices and you know how I hate to move. Anyway, let's not talk about that. Let's go get some dinner. I'm starving."

Starving? How could that be so? We've just seen Susan down two dozen powdered-sugar donuts in less than one hour. How could she possibly swallow another bite? Starving? Come on, you say. But starving is indeed what she is. Not for food, but for relief. Relief of pain, of loneliness, of anxiety, of frustration, of anger, sorrow, disappointment. Susan is a compulsive overeater or binger, and food is her solace. It's her means of regaining control, of coping with stress. It's an unhealthy and inappropriate one, but it's what she has come to rely on. She may binge in a manner much like a bulimic, but will rarely succumb to the need to purge afterward. The overeater's "purge" takes the form of continual rededication to "do better." In our case above, after the two dozen donuts and the big Mexican dinner, Susan will go to bed, numbed and stuffed to the gills. In the cold light of a new morning, however, she will likely wake up awash in a sea of guilt over having binged and will vow to the moon and the stars that she'll never do that again. She will promise herself not to give in to the urge to overeat; she'll have more willpower over it. But the promise probably won't stick, because the problem is infinitely more complicated than just a lack of willpower. The psychological and even physiologic needs that drive her to gorge often have little to do with being hungry. The food is a misused tool in a cycle of behavioral addiction—as it is for the bulimic and the anorectic—and until she discovers and corrects the underlying problem, the behavior will continue.

As a result, compulsive overeaters often become overweight to a significant degree, many gaining to BMI values in the 35 to 40 range or even higher (once again, see Table 1).

Unlike anorexia and bulimia, compulsive overeating has yet to secure an undisputed berth in formal psychiatric texts, and therefore the picture we can construct of it is hazier. It has been variously labeled *night-eaters syndrome* and *obese bulimia*, and just in the last few weeks as I am writing, new research into the disorder has labeled it *binge-eating disorder*.[7] Although the recognition of the disorder is certain, it is too newly labeled to be included in the authoritative book on the subject (DSM-III-R). Dr. Robert L. Spitzer, the researcher who has recently described the disorder before the Society of Behavioral Medicine in New York, has provided us with a neat list of the major characteristics[8] common to the disorder. These are:

1. Recurrent episodes of bingeing, and the sense that the eating is out of control.
2. Episodes occurring at least twice a week on average for six months.
3. The behavior causes marked distress.
4. Binges involve at least three of these actions:
   Eating much more rapidly than usual.
   Eating to uncomfortable fullness.
   Eating large amounts of food even when not hungry.
   Eating alone out of embarrassment.
   Feelings of disgust or guilt.

Although the syndrome has not yet received as careful research scrutiny as anorexia or bulimia, with the release of Dr. Spitzer's work the floodgates of research will surely open. Until that occurs, are we hamstrung in creating our portrait of the compulsive overeater or binge eater? Not entirely. Because many compulsive overeaters are obese, we can at least use the incidence and risks of obesity in general as a jumping-off spot. Certainly there are other causes of obesity—genetic causes and metabolic ones—but for a substantial number of those who become obese, bingeing plays at least some part. So who are the obese?

Vital Statistics: A Profile of Compulsive Overeaters, or Bingers

• *The overeater may be male or female.* And in this group, men may even outnumber women. In developed cultures, for every socioeconomic level there are more obese men than women except at the extremes of obesity, where it is roughly 50-50, at least in later years of life.

• *Lower socioeconomic groups tend to suffer from obesity* at six times the rate of more-affluent groups in developed countries, according to some studies. This reverse relationship of weight and wealth flip-flops in underdeveloped countries because of food scarcity. Under these conditions, affluence leads to obesity and poverty to thinness.

Also, among lower socioeconomic families a significant number of children qualify as obese by the age of six, which by all reckonings presages severe obesity in adulthood.[9] With regard to compulsive overeating behaviors, it may well be that overweight children learn to use food as a tool to cope with stresses of life from their parents (or others in the family) who do the same.

• *The overeaters—not unlike the anorectics—often suffer from an intense hatred of their body and a distortion of body image. But instead* of the overbearing focus anorectics have on the gain or loss of every ounce and in spending hours visually assessing the most minuscule pinch of each skin fold for hidden fat, the obese man or woman may go to the other extreme of purposefully avoiding stepping on a scale or looking into a mirror. Avoiding objective evidence of their increasing size allows overeaters to maintain the belief that the problem isn't all that bad. They're a bit overweight, yes, but *not obese*.

So, with these characteristics, we can begin to develop a sketchy picture of the compulsive overeater, the anorectic, and the bulimic. This information—indeed the whole point to this exercise—is offered with one clear purpose in mind: to help you to begin the process of freeing someone you love from their brand of self-destructive behavior.

Where to Begin to Help Someone You Love

So far, I've given you a general overview of the most basic characteristics common to disordered eaters of the three major types. You may recognize behaviors typical of one of these disorders in someone dear to you, perhaps even in yourself. But is that enough information for you to go on? Enough to make a "layman's diagnosis"? Should you dash out and confront the problem face-to-face right away? No, not yet, and probably not ever on your own. In the first place, with only the broad strokes I've painted so far, you may be hard-pressed to know whether you're correct in your suppositions or not. And second, even if you are right on the mark in your fears about your loved one's behavior, intervening in her behalf is not a one-person job. You will need lots of help to free your loved one from the eating disorder. Let me underscore at this point, lest I give the wrong impression, that the work you are about to undertake is difficult and emotionally trying at times. The road to freeing your loved one is not always going to be a smooth or easy one, but in the end, seeing your loved one whole and healthy will be your reward for the struggle.

The first step you must take is to speak with a professional counselor, preferably one well-versed in evaluating and treating eating disorders. This should not be planned as a meeting that includes the anorectic, bulimic, or overeater, but rather as a fact-gathering mission for you and anyone else interested in helping your loved one become free of her addiction to abnormal eating. Before you take any action that even indirectly confronts the disordered eater, get some guidance. Otherwise, you may find yourself making matters worse. The wrong move at this point could drive a wedge of mistrust between you and the person you're trying to help and could force her to even greater lengths to disguise or obscure the abnormality of her eating habits. The net result will almost certainly be to make your task more difficult.

The best resources for finding help will vary depending on the size and location of your community. With the rise in the incidence of eating disorders and the greater public awareness about them, many cities of even moderate size will have one or more psychiatric hospitals with established programs for the treatment of addictions of all types, including addictive eating behaviors. Likewise, because of the increased demand for such services, many general hospitals have developed both inpatient and outpatient programs to assist the disordered eater and her family. Under these circumstances, a telephone call can put you in touch with a knowledgeable counselor. Many such facilities even maintain dedicated "hot lines" to route incoming calls and answer questions.

In smaller towns, the local, county, or state mental health facility may provide such services or at least may be able to refer you to competent help. Failing that—or in addition to these facilities—there are a number of national organizations that can assist you. Here are two that should be able to assist you right away in taking that first step:

American Anorexia/Bulimia Association, Inc. (AABA)
418 E 76th St.
New York, New York 10021
(212) 734-1114
(Phone lines manned 9 A.M.–5 P.M. EST Monday–Friday)

National Association of Anorexia Nervosa and Associated Disorders (ANAD)
P.O. Box 7
Highland Park, Illinois 60035
(312) 831-3438

Both of these organizations maintain current national listings of therapists, counselors, physicians, and treatment facilities, and will refer you to a qualified specialist near you. Although their listings don't cover every corner of the globe, their referral base is broad, even including some foreign countries. (AA/BA has referral listings in England, Canada, Israel, and Spain.) Both organizations also publish national newsletters that you will find helpful and supportive, as well as educational materials on anorexia and bulimia.

If the loved one you are hoping to help suffers from compulsive overeating, look first to any local facilities that specialize in treating eating disorders in general. However, if you live in an area that doesn't have these kinds of services available, don't despair. Contact:

Overeaters Anonymous Headquarters
World Services Office
383 Van Ness Avenue, Suite 1601
Torrance, California 90501
(213) 618-8835

The national headquarters should be able to put you in touch with a local chapter in your general area. This group—like Alcoholics Anonymous, upon which it is based—is a voluntary organization in which former food addicts help current food addicts through the Twelve Steps to Recovery. Because it is operated and populated by recovering overeaters, the folks there are in an excellent position to give you names of reputable therapists, social workers, or other counselors in your area. Their firsthand experience will be invaluable to you in finding a knowledgeable professional to guide you.

Seeking First to Understand and Then to Help

Most of you have by now come to the realization—as Bill did when he discovered Ellen in the kitchen bingeing—that something is awry with your loved one's eating behavior. Perhaps at this point you're not entirely sure what that something is, only that it's not "normal." That realization brings with it a riot of emotions: you may be fearful, mystified, confused, frustrated, angry, or all of these in some measure. The bizarreness of an eating disorder—in a person whom you have until now viewed as stable, solid, responsible—may tempt you to think you can just march in and talk some sense into her, and that she will respond with some variant on the old *slap slap,* *"Thanks, I needed that"* routine. I can assure you that nothing could be further from the truth. No amount of pleading and persuasion at this point will make her understand. And so, it's up to you to do the understanding.

Now is a time for you to strive to understand her, the disorder, and her reasons for succumbing to it. To be in a position to help, you must educate yourself, and you must try to appreciate the forces that drive her disorder. You must try to put yourself into her skin, into her mind, and once there to understand what she's trying to accomplish by doing what she does. Begin to recognize that her problem is much bigger than a bizarre eating pattern;

the restriction, bingeing, or purging is nothing more than a tool she's using to cope with a bigger, deeper stress.

Your interview with a therapist or counselor is your first step in beginning to understand her problem. It is imperative that you take that first step, because right now, she probably cannot.

Your goals in visiting with the counselor should be fivefold:

1. Be open and honest. Describe as honestly and fully as you are able the symptoms you have seen in your friend or relative that lead you to fear she is in the grip of an abnormal eating behavior. Don't be afraid to say what you know or have surmised, even if it casts yourself or another family member or friend in a bad light. Remember, the health or even the life of someone you love may rest on your being honest about the circumstances. Your privacy and that of your loved ones is safe; a licensed counselor will—in fact, must—hold this information in strictest confidence. But only by giving the counselor the full story as you know it can you hope to come away from this interview with any useful information.

2. Ask the counselor to direct you to as much information about the disorder as possible, and immerse yourself in it. Take care at this point not to flaunt the information before your loved one. Doing so could push you into a confrontation about the behavior that neither of you is yet prepared to have.

3. Ask the counselor whether he or she thinks the behavior you have described constitutes grounds for concern. And if so, what kind and how serious a problem does it appear at present to be?

4. Ask the counselor for guidance in how to proceed next. He or she may want to spend a few more visits with you to help solidify your understanding of the problem and to help deal with your fears and concerns as well. Or perhaps the therapist would like to meet with other family members to begin the process of sorting out whether some family situation has triggered the abnormal eating behavior. For example, perhaps there's been a divorce or separation, a health problem, or a death in the family that has created a major emotional stress.

5. Together with the counselor, discuss when and how to reveal your suspicions and fears to your loved one. In some instances, the counselor might suggest an interview with the disordered eater right away—if she agrees to it. If the disordered eater is a young teenager—such as Lindsey—and she objects, you may have to insist that she attend the session. The situation is a little stickier when the disordered eater is an adult—like Ellen or Susan. In a later section when we discuss how to conduct an intervention, we'll look at some approaches you can take to help improve the chances that she will agree to at least an initial interview.

I have said that your first task is to begin to understand the problem, so let's shift gears now and examine the psychological forces at work in anorexia, bulimia, and compulsive overeating or binge-eating disorder.

Chapter Two

The Making of a Disordered Eater

Although the incidence of the symptoms that modern medicine has dubbed eating disorders has exploded in the last several decades, the behaviors themselves have been documented for centuries. Anorexia, especially, has been traced as far back as the Middle Ages to such historically important figures as Saint Catherine of Siena, who, it was said, ate no food but partook only of the Holy Eucharist (the wine and the wafer) in passionate devotion to her religion.

From the Middle Ages (thirteenth through sixteenth centuries) through the middle of the nineteenth century, experts (mainly clergy) declared such extreme demonstrations of faith and piety to be proof that such women—and throughout history the disorder does occur almost exclusively in women—were miraculous beings, not bound by the needs of the flesh. Indeed, some people even believed these famous anorectics to be not of the flesh at all, but purely spiritual and therefore not requiring normal, mortal sustenance—i.e., food.

The rarity of this condition, referred to at that time as *anorexia mirabilis*, generated such publicity that people from far and wide would flock to see the fasting woman of Tutbury; or Mollie Fancher, the fasting girl of Brooklyn; or the Derbyshire Damsel.

The publicity, the constant attention, and at times even financial benefit that accrued to the families of the "marvelous maids" of history may have played at least some role in perpetuating the sense of miraculousness that surrounded their self-starvation. However, not everyone believed the maids' claims of eating or drinking nothing for years to be miraculous. A substantial cadre of skeptics—usually intellectuals or medical experts of the period—devoted their time to proving them to be frauds and phonies, setting up round-the-clock watches to discover how they secretly ate or drank. The investigators reaped their expected reward by rooting out some (often minuscule) hidden source of food in many cases, but in others, they could verify only that the fasting girl took nothing during their vigil.

In one such case—that of Sarah Jacobs of Wales, reputed not to have eaten a bite in twenty-six months—it became apparent to the medical investigators that she was dying from her efforts to prove her case. They pleaded with the parents to call the vigil off and to take her to a hospital to be fed, but the Jacobses steadfastly refused, convinced beyond reason that their daughter's claim was legitimate. The vigil continued, but two weeks without water in a body already emaciated by prolonged food and fluid restriction proved too much for her. Sarah Jacobs died. Ultimately, the authorities charged her father, Evan Jacobs, with criminal negligence in not compelling his daughter to eat.[1]

Whatever motivation sparked their behavior, anorectics certainly appeared with fair regularity from the Middle Ages onward, and usually with some religious or spiritualistic claim. But what of this century? The sacred overtones have all but vanished, as have the attendant local publicity and potential for financial gain; what new reasons can we discover to explain the explosion of this kind of behavior among today's young women?

Three Theories on the Development of Eating Disorders

Experts in the field of psychiatry try to develop theories—sometimes called theoretical models—to explain why a disorder occurs. The researchers look for some basic connection, some common denominator among the cases, not only to help them better understand the disorder itself, but in many cases to give insight into who might be at risk to develop the disorder and what might reduce that risk. In the case of the eating disorders, research has centered on three major theoretical models: the psychodynamic, the sociocultural, and the biological. Let's examine each briefly.

The psychodynamic model holds that some abnormality in childhood or some disruption in the family dynamics of the anorectic or bulimic (not as much work has been done on compulsive overeating in this model yet) leads her to develop bizarre eating behaviors to mask, repress, or otherwise control the situation. For example, one group of psychodynamic theorists offered the explanation that anorexia nervosa represented the fear of becoming pregnant by eating, with bulimia representing the other side of the coin—i.e., a fantasy of becoming pregnant through overeating.[2] And along a similar line, the practitioners in the late 1800s viewed anorexic behavior as an attempt by the faster to forestall sexual maturity, fertility—in effect, to remain in adolescence.

In recent years, these hypotheses have given way to other theories that focus more on abnormalities in family dynamics and interrelationships. For example, in bulimia more than the other disorders, clinicians often uncover drug and alcohol addiction in parents or other family members, or abusive behaviors that not uncommonly include sexual abuse. The psychodynamic theorists might tend to describe this kind of family setting as chaotic, unstable, even violent. On the other hand, they might describe the "typical" family of an anorexic patient as being overinvolved with one another or perhaps overcontrolling, or as having an interdependency that creates an environment in which the child cannot develop a sense of her own bodily needs. Perhaps she cannot do so because there is no need; someone else has always told her what to do and when.

I recall just such a situation in an acquaintance—I'll call her Deena here—from my high school. She was the only child of a couple slightly older than most of our parents, and they seemed to adore her, showering her with chic clothes, a car, stereos, jewelry. But despite all these outward signs of love, even to my untrained teenage eye the relationship between Deena and her parents—especially her mother—seemed odd. What I noticed was that her mother did everything for her, including things she, as a high school senior, should certainly have been more than capable of doing herself. Deena's mother would decide what she would wear, laying out her clothes for her every night. When Deena left the house with a group of friends for a football game, her mother would not hand her money, even if she held her hand out to take it, but would rather put it into her jacket pocket and snap it closed for her, as you might a first-grade child's. I remember once Deena popped the button on the waist of her shorts, laughing. Her mother sent her to get a safety pin from the back of the house. When she came back into the room, she had begun to pin the waistband closed. Her mother practically shrieked out, "Give me that pin, Deena, *I* will do it for you."

Deena was a pretty girl with a gorgeous figure, a cheerleader, time and again elected homecoming royalty by the school, quite personable and popular with her classmates, intelligent, but nonetheless a prisoner of her mother's control. Probably in large measure because of her mother's overwhelming degree of protectiveness, she became anorectic. As is the case with most disordered eaters, their rebellion with food is often their only one, but only they, ultimately, can control what or whether they eat. They may stand for having their clothes selected, their friends chosen, even their shorts pinned back together as if they were good little five-year-old girls. But when it comes to the bottom line, control of this one thing—food—is theirs alone. The power they feel from wresting back control over even this tiny corner of their lives can be phenomenal. It can become like a drug to the psyche and, for some young women, evolve into an addictive behavior that can become both a torture and an ecstasy simultaneously.

To my knowledge, Deena's eating disorder lasted only briefly and did not recur, although we lost touch long ago. However, relapse into abnormal eating behaviors under stress is not an uncommon problem. I've often thought about Deena, especially during the writing of this book, and wondered how she's fared over time. Although I feel that her mother's need to control every aspect of Deena's life led to the development of the eating disorder, what has puzzled me most is what caused her mother to do it. She seemed to love Deena, and I don't think she ever meant consciously to hurt her; it just seemed to grow out of an abnormal family protectiveness.

A part of the abnormality in their family situation perhaps arose because Deena's mother was morbidly obese, weighing on the order of 300 pounds, my trained eye would now guess. Perhaps she was a compulsive overeater, or perhaps she suffered from some endocrine (glandular) abnormality, but whatever the cause of her obesity, she must have also felt imprisoned. She rarely ever left their house. And when she did—even if it was August in Arkansas in the dog days, she went out swathed in ankle-length, muumuu-style dresses, with a coat, a scarf, and sunglasses. Her obvious discomfort with her own body image—especially if she was a compulsive overeater and felt herself powerless against a desire to binge—may have spawned in her a fierce desire to "save" her daughter from the same fate. Ironically, she propelled Deena toward a different, but equally unpleasant, one.

From the vantage point I now have as a physician who has seen and studied these disorders, what amazes me most is that Deena was able to recover quickly, and that the anorexia was short-lived. Deena's case may not be a typical one, but the developmental circumstances of her disorder serve nicely to illustrate a classic case of the psychodynamic theory.

But a psychodynamic model is only one slant on the possible causes of disordered eating. Some psychiatric theorists favor a sociocultural model instead, which attributes the development of eating disorders to the pressures of our culture and society on young women. I mentioned earlier the emphasis that the media (and society as a whole) place on super-thinness in women. It is just this kind of cultural expectation that proponents of the sociocultural model point to as causative in the startling rise of disordered eating in recent years. One group even conducted a study of *Playboy* models and Miss America contestants over the last twenty years to document that, in both groups, the young women have become steadily and significantly thinner. It is these women, of course, whom the media and entertainment industry hold out as the standard or norm, but who in reality most likely fall somewhere on the upward tail of the large bell curve of women's weights, shapes, and sizes, representing the thinnest 3 to 5 percent of women. But it is toward this ideal that America's women aspire. A recent Gallup poll sponsored by the American Dietetic Association revealed that 44 percent of women feel guilty about eating their favorite foods.[3] These kinds of feelings create a love-hate relationship with food that pervades female thought across all age groups. But especially during the teen years, at a vulnerable time in a young woman's life when peer approval and appearance matter more to her than her health, she may fall into a pattern of abnormal eating in a misguided effort to attain some unrealistic shape or size.

Bending to conform to such cultural forces, then, becomes the basis for a sociocultural explanation of anorexia or bulimia, but does that offer much insight into compulsive overeating? Surely, no one can believe that a young woman would stuff herself with food to the point of weighing 200 or 300 pounds in an effort to conform to a cultural mandate for thinness. Or would she?

What if, in an effort to reduce a plump figure to become more "acceptable" in the eyes of her peers, a young girl vowed to restrict herself to an unrealistically low number of calories? Then what if the attendant hunger she experienced finally drove her to eat—or overeat—and she gained a little more? That would naturally be followed by another, more fervent, vow to even more severely restrict herself. But again, what if she could not "stick with it" and broke her vow and binged on the foods she'd been missing? What if, little by little, her weight crept upward to a point that a little bit of dieting would do no good, and she felt more and more helpless, hopeless, and trapped? At that point, she might begin to feel that it was useless to try, and that she might as well eat because at least she enjoyed that. But in no time, television and movies would plaster the image of the newest svelte star or model everywhere she looked, and she'd be back to trying to diet, falling off the wagon and bingeing, and gaining some more weight. So, in theory at least, we could envision how trying to conform and failing could ultimately lead to compulsive overeating. But could there be other forces at work? Sure.

And that brings us to the final of the major theories of disorder eating behavior: the biological one. The research currently under way on this subject would fill its own book, but I will try to distill the major areas under study for you.

The research into a biological cause for the eating disorders has primarily focused on aberrations of brain chemicals called *neurotransmitters*. You can think of these substances as chemical messengers, released by particular parts of the brain in response to certain stimuli. Once set free, these neurotransmitters travel to other parts of the brain to relay their given message by interacting with structures called *neuroreceptors*. When the messenger arrives, it passes a preset message to that area of the brain; the message it would transmit to some other area of the brain might be the exact opposite one. The neuroreceptors in a given area of brain function like a radio receiver set to pick up only one channel. They hear the message they've been programmed to hear, and all others pass by unheard.

The site of action of these messengers is an area of the brain called the *hypothalamus*. Anatomists further subdivide the hypothalamus into even smaller sections called *nuclei*, among which reside two structures you may already have heard of: the feeding center and the satiety center. Messages arriving in these centers normally tell us we're hungry and need to eat (the feeding center) or that we've eaten plenty and should stop before we get too full (the satiety center). It is malfunction of the messengers or message receivers within these brain areas that researchers believe may form the biological basis for the major eating disorders. An avalanche of research, some already completed and some currently under way, may soon give us some clear answers about what these abnormalities are and what could correct them.

With regard to feeding behavior, research has already shown that several neurotransmitters play critical roles in the brain: norepinephrine (NE), dopamine (DA), serotonin (also called 5-hydroxytryptamine, or 5HT), and neuropeptide Y (NPY). Let's take a look at each to see how it should work normally, and then examine what, if any, aberrations the research has suggested to explain disordered eating behavior.

Norepinephrine (NE)

This neurotransmitter is the chemical cousin of epinephrine, a substance you may be familiar with by its other name, adrenalin. These two neurotransmitters (NE and epi) function throughout the body in a variety of ways, most notably in the "fight or flight" response that causes the changes in blood pressure, breathing, pulse rate, and sense of readiness that comes over us when we become frightened, startled, or anxious. These are the messengers responsible for making our "blood boil" when we get angry.

In the hypothalamus, however, they (especially NE) serve a different function. An outpouring (or "spike," in medical parlance) of NE traveling to the feeding center causes a desire to eat—and a preference for carbohydrate-rich food, i.e., sugars and starches. The signals that normally stimulate the spike include such physiologic states as hunger and falling blood sugar, among others. In the disordered eater, the spike may occur from an outpouring of NE because of stress, fear, anxiety, or by some mechanism we have not as yet recognized.

Once the feeding center receives the "need to eat" message, if we're in a position to do so, we eat. If the system works according to plan, the meal then stimulates the release of other neurotransmitters (notably serotonin, about which we'll talk next), which functions to quiet the NE message and to shut off the desire to eat.

Studies on untreated anorectic patients have verified that these women have low levels of the breakdown products of NE compared to controls.[4] These levels seem to return to normal after refeeding and weight gain, which leads us to wonder which came first, low levels of NE or anorexia? It is tempting to hypothesize that since NE plays a critical role in transmitting the "need to eat" signal under normal conditions, low levels of it would blunt the signal to eat. A defect such as this could be the triggering stimulus behind the development of anorexic behavior in some women. So far, it is only a tempting hypothesis. Research has not given us a clear answer about this issue, but the work proceeds apace.

Serotonin (5HT)

When the chemical messenger system functions as it should, this neurotransmitter acts on neuroreceptors in the satiety center to signal us to quit eating. A heavy dose of carbohydrate-rich foods causes the brain to release 5HT, which then goes to work turning off the craving for carbohydrates and turning on a preference for protein-rich and fatty foods. Once the levels of 5HT reach sufficient proportions in the hypothalamic satiety center, desire for more food of any kind wanes, and our brain tells us to stop, that we're "full."

Research has shown a clearer connection for abnormalities of 5HT or insensitivity of its receptors as a biologic basis for bingeing than for any of the other neurotransmitters or eating disorders.[5] The thinking is that aberrations in the functioning of these 5HT feedback control circuits to say "enough, already" may be what's gone haywire or short-circuited. And this makes perfect sense. If the stress stimulus (the NE spike) that starts the feeding cycle going works, but the feedback control that turns the process off once it's activated is sluggish or fails to kick in—if that one channel radio isn't tuned properly—the message to stop eating would never get through. So it may be with the bulimic and compulsive overeater; a biologic short circuit may contribute to their eating disorder.

Once researchers get on the trail of such a defect, it's often just a short leap to their figuring out how to get around it. And so it may be with the 5HT defect. There are already volumes of research on several promising drugs that may correct or at least control this defect. What that would mean is a discovery nothing short of miraculous for the many people who wrestle with an uncontrollable urge to binge. But more about the drug therapies and the frontiers of new research and hope later on. For now, let's get back to the other neurotransmitters.

Neuropeptide Y (NPY)

Energy deprivation—food/calorie restriction so commonly seen in all the eating disorders—causes an outpouring of the chemical messenger NPY. Although restriction is not the only stimulator to its release, with regard to the development of bingeing it may be of paramount importance. Once released, NPY primarily acts in concert with NE in helping to stimulate the desire to eat, and again, especially to eat carbohydrate-rich foods. NPY also seems to blunt the release of 5HT, thereby delaying the signal to make the switch to protein—an action that tends to prolong the urge to eat carbohydrates—and diminishing the signal that says "stop eating."

Here, as in the case of 5HT, medical studies have detected disturbances in the balance of NPY in the brain fluid in patients with anorexia and bulimia. The significance of these disturbances remains unclear at this point. Interestingly, however, other research implicates a possible relationship between rising NPY levels in the hypothalamus, the onset of puberty, and the development of adult eating patterns, at least in young female rats. The research suggests a connection between these behavioral and glandular events that could help to uncover another link between disturbances in biology and the development of eating disorders in human subjects.

The Endogenous Opiates

When the discovery of natural narcoticlike substances in the body, called the endorphins and enkephalins, garnered researchers the Nobel prize, medical investigative teams went to work to uncover what roles these substances played. Since that time, medical science has shown that we release these natural opiates in response to such stimuli as pain and fear. These substances are what's behind those tales that you may have heard tales of a mother picking up a tree to free her trapped child, or the soldier carrying a wounded mate two miles while hobbling on a fractured leg. Nature has protected us from catastrophic pain by endowing us with these natural narcotics. But their release may do more than merely blunt pain; it may impart a sensation of pleasure, not unlike their synthetic relatives the synthetic opiates (such drugs as heroin, morphine, and codeine). It is the pleasurable quality that probably accounts for the "high" that runners or chronic exercisers feel when they reach a certain point in their workout. Nice to know, you say, but what does all this have to do with eating disorders? Possibly plenty. Let me explain.

Some research indicates that bulimic patients who purge through vomiting show increased levels of beta-endorphin, one of the natural opiates. The increase may come from the stress of vomiting, or it may occur in response to the high caloric intake, but whatever its source, it may be partly responsible for the pleasurable, calming effect that most bulimic vomiters equate with the act. Using vomiting to induce a feeling of calm apparently occurs in nonbulimic people, such as entertainers before going on stage or women with severe menstrual cramps who use it to blunt the pain.[6]

But in the disordered eater, inducing a heightened state of natural opiate outpouring may only drive her to more binge eating: research has long ago recognized the opiates (both the body's naturally occurring ones as well as the store-bought variety) as appetite stimulants in virtually all mammalian species, including the human. Food deprivation (such as severely restrictive diets inadequate to support nutritional needs) also causes measurable rises in beta-endorphin in the hypothalamus. Other research has shown that opiates not only increase feeding in general, but also alter taste selection, causing a preference for sweet and fat foods.

This association between opiates and appetite has, naturally, led researchers to wonder whether the opiate blockers (the most famous of which is the drug naloxone, which is currently available to treat narcotics overdoses) might blunt the appetite. And indeed they appear to do just that, suppressing both the desire to eat as well as the preference for sweets and fat.[7] Further research into this area may ultimately provide us with medications that control the bingeing urge for bulimics and compulsive overeaters, or help to normalize the suppressed appetite in anorectics.

Combining the Models

Although each of these models has merit on its own, I favor, instead, the model or theory described by Joan Jacobs Brumberg in *Fasting Girls: The History of Anorexia Nervosa*[8] that combines parts of all the three major theories. She refers to this model with regard to anorexia (which is the subject of her book) as "addiction to starving." I'd like to expand on that definition to include the other major disorders as well and call it "addiction to disordered eating." In my experience, this combined-model explanation seems to make the most sense.

The progression from normalcy to disorder in this "addiction to" model follows three defined stages: The first stage is recruitment, in which the young woman may begin to innocently restrict her intake of food or flirt with purging for psychological, social, or cultural reasons. Then comes the acclimation stage, during which she may not only become accustomed to the feelings of hunger, nutritional deprivation, satiety from bingeing, or relief from purging, but actually experience some sort of satisfaction mediated through the endogenous opiates, like the "high" that runners experience.[9] Then, for some biologically susceptible individuals, if abnormalities in brain chemicals scramble the normal controls of appetite, the situation becomes chronic, and a dependence on the behavior, like an addiction to a drug, develops. Let me apply this kind of model to a few cases and see if it also makes sense to you. First, let's set a few ground rules.

We must begin by assuming that there indeed *are* biological differences between those young women who develop eating disorders and the rest of the population that does not. Let's further suppose that these biological variations create the *potential* to cause imbalances or other abnormalities in brain chemicals controlling appetite (suppression for anorectics and stimulation for bulimics and compulsive overeaters) under certain conditions. Let's agree to accept these theories as fact for the purposes of our model, even though such relationships have not yet been proved conclusively.

Onto this susceptible biological framework, let's then add a catalyst of psychological, social, or cultural stress. For example, let's add the stress of a puberty growth spurt, with the natural increase in body fat and change of body image that come with it. Let's look back at the example of Lindsey, the anorectic teenager I introduced you to in Chapter 1, and apply this model to her case.

When Lindsey was in ninth grade, puberty rounded her out into what her mother described as "a little pudgy" (a socio-cultural no-no). At this critical time, being a little pudgy drives many young women to thoughts of dieting, and Lindsey was no different. She began to restrict her intake of calories for socio-cultural reasons—i.e., she had been *recruited* into the behavior. Once recruited, she pursued the behavior with greater vigor, enjoying the sense of control and power she felt over her body, until she reached the point that she didn't feel hungry even though all she'd eaten in a day was a couple of grapes and three crackers. Lindsey had become *acclimated* to the pangs of hunger that would normally signal a need to eat. When she said she didn't need to eat, from her perspective she was telling the truth. Even though her weight had fallen off to a sufficient degree to be noticeable (and worrisome) to her parents, and even in the face of developing nutritional deficiencies, the fasting had dulled her physiologic drive to eat. Like the "marvelous maids" of history, Lindsey had come to honestly think she didn't need to eat. Her brain no longer listened to biologic urges to feed, perhaps because the potential for chemical imbalances that we spoke of earlier had become a reality under the stimulus of the fasting or starved state. Perhaps alterations in brain chemicals that should have signaled a need to eat no longer functioned normally to warn her of impending disaster. Instead, she received haywire signals that suffused her with a sense of satisfaction, satiety, and even euphoria instead of hunger and anxiety. If such chemical aberrations are the case—and we've agreed to assume that to be true—then they could lead her down the road to *dependency* on this behavior. In effect, she would become addicted to starving unless someone intervened to free her.

So the "addiction to" model seems to adequately explain a case like Lindsey's anorexia. But what about bulimia? Would the model explain why Ellen wound up cross-legged on the kitchen floor in the middle of the night, cupcake and peanut butter in hand? Let's try it out and see.

Recall that Ellen and her husband Bill were a two-career couple that seemed to have it all together, to be on the sure track to success and happiness, destined to live out the great American dream. But under the surface or in their past, what lay unseen? Let me give you the rest of her story.

Ellen grew up in a suburb of a large midwestern city, one of four children, but the only daughter, of a strict Irish Protestant family. Every morning, her father left for the plant where he worked as a foreman on the line. Every evening, he stopped on his way home at the local bar to unwind. Many nights, he came home loud and drunk, cursing and railing across the dinner table at anyone who crossed him, which the boys too often did. But not little Ellen. She had seen up close what happened when you crossed Daddy. So she learned early in life to be quiet and polite, to stay out of his way, to be sure all her things were picked up, to always make good grades, to never talk back. In short, to be as perfect as she could be. She felt if she could be good enough, maybe the drunkenness would stop.

Sometimes, when her father went on a rampage, she would slip up to her bedroom, close the door, and wait it out. Then, later, when the house was quiet—usually that meant Daddy had finally burned himself out and gone to bed—she would slip down to the kitchen and sit alone in the dark on the floor by the refrigerator and eat. She would stuff herself with whatever came to hand, going through entire loaves of bread, bags of cookies, jars of peanut butter, until she felt the numbness wrap around her, blocking out the memory of her father's anger. Then, when she felt that almost pleasant sensation of stretching in her stomach, she would drink down a quart or more of milk and wait. Before long, she would tiptoe back upstairs to the bathroom in the hall and make herself vomit and vomit and vomit, until all the food was gone. Then she would flush the toilet and pretend that all the bad things within her and her family that caused Daddy to feel all the rage had come out, too, and were also going down the drain. And she would feel like everything would be better.

She had begun to binge and purge occasionally at age fifteen, but as her father's alcoholism worsened and the abusive evenings became more frequent, so did Ellen's "secret cure" for it. By the time she entered high school, her "cure" helped her control other stresses, as well.

Now that you have a fuller picture of Ellen's past, can we explain her entry into bulimia using the "addiction to" model? Let's give it a try. Again, we have to allow ourselves to accept that there is indeed some sort of underlying biological susceptibility that under the right set of circumstances can trigger incorrect chemical need-to-feed signals in the brain. But once we've made that leap, the rest is easy.

Here was a young girl, a "good" girl, a pleaser, living on the edge of the maelstrom of her father's drunken rage. She probably felt frightened and alone in a situation she had no control over, never knowing when he would come home drunk, never sure when her brothers or her mother would overstep the shifting boundaries of his anger and set it off. Instability of this nature places a horrendous psychological burden on a young mind. The stress of not knowing what's going to happen from day to day or even minute to minute sends even adults with inadequate abilities to cope running to alcohol, to drugs, to the therapist. How much greater a weight does this kind of stress place on a young girl?

Then, once suffering under this psychic strain, what if Ellen reacted one night by creeping down to the kitchen, where it's usually warm, and quiet, and filled with welcome smells? You've probably felt that impulse yourself. How many of us have not at one time or another in our lives felt comforted and soothed after a disappointment by someone's offer of a batch of warm cookies and some milk? Or relaxed over a brownie and a hot steaming cup of coffee after a stressful day? How many of us have promised our children ice cream or candy if they would be "good" at the doctor's office? Using food as a reward for behavior or a solace during stress is standard operating procedure for many families. So it shouldn't seem all that unusual that Ellen sought quiet and comfort there.

What happened next was that she discovered she could blot out her feelings and emotions with food, just as her father did with liquor. And here is where the biological short circuit comes in. Normally, we eat until we are full, then stop. But if the chemical signals that tell our brain we're full don't work properly, we can go on. Perhaps it was so with Ellen. She could eat and eat and eat, focusing only on the food and the lack of feeling until she was beyond stuffed and felt nothing. Then, in an act of her own will, her control, she could undo the whole thing by vomiting. She could purge herself of the bad feelings, expel them, get rid of them. Once she made this discovery, she had been *recruited* into the bulimic behavior. When she later began to use her "secret cure" regularly to cope with stresses at school and in interpersonal relationships outside the family, she had *acclimated*. And then, finally, when she couldn't cope day to day without bingeing and purging, she had become *dependent* on the "cure." Ellen became addicted to her eating disorder as a means of coping with stress, just as her father had become addicted to alcohol, and probably for the same reason.

And so, for Ellen, abnormal family psychodynamics provided the impetus for her development of bulimia, but the biologic susceptibility probably had to be there first.

Strange Eating Behaviors Do Not Constitute Disorders

Children—teenagers, especially—can develop unusual behaviors related to what they will or will not eat. For example, I remember my youngest son at about the age of four announcing that he would no longer eat raisins. He had enjoyed them regularly up until that point in his lunches or in the afternoon, but suddenly, no go. Since raisins were the only fruit item, unless you can count orange juice, that he would ever eat to begin with, his refusal concerned us. After many weeks of intermittently questioning him about why he had sworn off raisins, he finally told me they had "baby sticks and baby rocks in them" and he wouldn't eat them again. Apparently, he had gotten a batch with a few seeds and stems in it, which to him appeared to be rocks and sticks, and that was all she wrote on the subject. No more raisins for him! He is now fourteen, and he still won't willingly eat fruit except orange juice, so we get our fiber and vitamins in other ways. His behavior, to me, qualifies as weird—I mean, who ever heard of a kid that didn't like some kind of fruit?—but it's not disordered. It's a matter of personal taste preference.

Many children and teens don't develop a taste for some vegetables until they're grown. It's probably more the rule than the exception that the vegetables kids will eat include potatoes, beans, corn, rice, and pasta. Don't even try for zucchini, beets, sweet potatoes, asparagus, broccoli, or little green peas. These are developmental refusals and are not disordered. They'll grow out of it. Parents can often get around these refusals by compromise, without making a federal case out of their distaste in much the same way my own mother did. The house rule for edibles one didn't like was to take "just a taste to be polite." For small countable things, the magic number in our household was nine. I remember as a child counting out nine green peas, nine lima beans, nine pieces of squash. It was a compromise we could all live with, so meals could be a time for conversation and sharing of ideas and tales, not a nutritional battlefield.

Some teens and preteens go through phases that involve positioning of food on the plate or a defined order of eating it. For example, they might prefer that none of the dishes on their plate touch—i.e., no intermingling of the mashed potatoes and the green beans. Or they might feel that they need to eat one dish at a time—first all the peas, then all the squash, then all the chicken. Strange? I would agree that it is. But disordered? Probably not, although peculiar habits with food arrangement commonly occur in anorexia, such as cutting the food into tiny pieces or moving it around on the plate. Anorectics, however, usually don't *eat* the food, and therein lies the difference.

When I was a child, I preferred not to eat anything with "strings and lumps"—which meant coconut and nuts—in it. Many adolescent and teenage girls develop a finicky attitude about what's OK to eat and what's not. Often, these changes reflect some new bit of information they've discovered. For example, some youngsters refuse milk for a time upon learning that it comes from the udders of cows and not a plastic jug at the store. I know a woman who never did get over her aversion to milk on these precise grounds. And often, in their teen years, as they begin to develop a social consciousness of sorts, many young women will engage in "boycott refusal" of such foods as veal or tuna, or occasionally even become vegetarian for a time, because they cannot bear the thought of where the meat comes from and the cruel methods used to obtain it. Should you worry if your child engages in this kind of eating behavior? Not necessarily. These food-related behaviors may seem unusual, abnormal, even downright unreasonable, but they are probably not disordered. So where do we draw the line between strangeness and sickness? Between unusual and disordered? Between a phase and a problem?

Stepping Across the Line

The basic difference between strange habits and disordered ones rests in the reason behind the behavior. Young women will often go through "spells" of odd eating habits, or will even briefly flirt with dieting, food restricting, or even purging behaviors in a social way. By that I mean, influenced by friends who engage in this kind of eating behavior, she may indulge in a bit of it herself to fit in. Such experimentation may not be cause for alarm; however, be aware that it may inadvertently introduce a triggering stimulus to a biologically susceptible young woman and thus recruit her into a pattern of disordered eating.

Behavior that begins innocently crosses the line into disorder when the food or the behavior concerning it becomes a means of coping. When a young woman responds to the stress of an upcoming test, a poor performance, a disappointment at school, or the grief of a loss by retreating into a binge/purge or restrictive pattern of eating, the behavior is disordered. When attempting to control her stress, anxiety, fear, or rage prompts the strange behaviors—to avoid eating with the family, to eat in a ritualistic way, to overeat at night, to shun broad food categories—the behavior becomes a substitute for the development of normal, healthy coping skills, and a barrier to normal growth and maturity. And the specter of disordered eating rears its head.

What Drives the Disordered Eater?

Naturally, the specific reasons that cause young women to develop eating disorders vary from person to person. However, there are a few common threads that weave their way time and again into the stories these women relate during the course of therapy. Let's catch the ends of these threads and see if they will help us to unravel some of the whys of disordered eating behavior.

Numbing the Pain

Bulimics and compulsive overeaters consistently report achieving a sense of numbness or blunting of their emotions from binge eating. During the binge, disordered eaters seem to apply food like a soothing, anesthetic balm to a raw psyche, pouring on more and more until it doesn't hurt anymore. As I have previously described, this pain relieving effect occurs through the stimulation of natural opiate release. But what causes the pain in the first place? The specific reasons for a particular woman's psychic anguish can in reality be large or small, including anything from a scholastic, personal, or business disappointment, to failure to meet self-imposed demands to achieve some unrealistic (or very difficult) goal, to the breakdown of an interpersonal relationship, to something as heinous as her suffering (or having suffered) emotional, physical, or sexual abuse. The bulimic or compulsive overeater uses food like a drug to mask the pain, and as a tool to give her a sense (albeit a false one) of being in control of the situation. The anorectic rigidly restricts her appetite and denies her hunger to reap a similar psychic reward: controlling what is—or seems to her to be—uncontrollable.

Filling the Void

Disordered eaters, like people with depression, often describe feeling a sense of emptiness or purposelessness that gnaws away like a hunger in their soul. Feeding that hunger—quite literally, in the case of bingers—most likely works through the release of brain chemicals (opiates, serotonin, or another brain chemical, called dopamine, that we did not discuss before) to leave them with a transient sense of euphoria or well-being. In the case of restrictive anorectics, the stress of fasting and high levels of metabolic breakdown products that come about from little or no intake of food also engender a euphoric sensation. The disordered eater, then, opts for transient false euphoria over psychic emptiness. She fills the void in her soul artificially through food or starvation.

Elevating Mood

I have said that the disordered eater uses food like a drug. In this sense, bingeing in bulimics and overeaters and fasting in anorectics are nothing more than forms of self-medication to control pain, anxiety, fear, boredom, loneliness, depression, and guilt. Over the past decade or so, a substantial amount of research into the relationship between human emotion and the excessive intake of high-calorie, carbohydrate-rich foods has emerged. Most of this work centers around the theory that some disorders of mood—depression, seasonal affective disorder,[10] pre-menstrual syndrome, and compulsive overeating (referred to as carbohydrate-craving obesity)—may occur because of abnormally low levels of serotonin (5HT) in the brain. Low levels of this neurotransmitter cause not only depression, but anxiety, irritability, and sleep disturbances. Their hypothesis is that the sufferer attempts to self-medicate to relieve the alteration of mood (the depression, anxiety, anger, or whatever) by eating foods that will cause the release of serotonin.[11] Instead of taking a mood-elevating drug, the binger engages in what she has come to recognize as a mood-elevating behavior.

The anorectic, on the other hand, uses fasting as a tool to

elevate her mood. Her psychic reward probably occurs through the increase in beta-endorphins (the natural opiates), which impart a sense of euphoria or well-being, or from the ketones in the blood, which can do the same.

Validating the Self

Disordered eaters of all three types share a common bond. They lack the normal degree of self-worth. These feelings of worthlessness or inadequacy can develop for a variety of reasons. Perhaps their family setting failed to allow them to develop an appropriate sense of their own ability and value; perhaps it was one that fostered too much dependence. A restrictive, overcontrolling, overprotective environment may hamper self-reliance and may impair the development of healthy coping skills. A chaotic, erratic, unstable, or frankly unsafe environment can put a child into a position of responsibility too great for her to handle. The former setting seems to occur more frequently in the families of anorectics and the latter in the families of bulimics, but there are no absolutes. In either event, the young woman may come to equate worthiness with thinness. It is no surprise that the young women of today might come to think that thinness equals worth, when this message blares out from every television, radio, newsstand, and movie theater in the country.

And in a disordered eater, even in the face of what appears to the outsider as success—high academic honors, athletic awards, career success, physical beauty—she may feel herself to be a total failure in every facet of her life, excluding control of her weight. Her own fragile self-worth may be so intimately tied to success in controlling her weight that her personal sense of value bobs like a cork on a rough sea with weight fluctuations as small as a fraction of a pound.

Living in Quiet Desperation

Couple this kind of thinking about the value of thinness our society places on its women with an uncontrollable urge to eat, perhaps on biological grounds, and you may begin to get some appreciation of the tortures and anguish that many bulimics and compulsive overeaters live with every waking minute of every day.

But what of the restrictive anorectic, who is not given to binges or purges? Does she suffer these tortures as well? The answer to that is probably yes—and no. Yes, most anorectics experience extreme anguish over every ounce, every perceived morsel of fat they might find, because they value thinness perhaps to the greatest degree of all. They truly feel they can't be thin enough—even at an emaciated 90 pounds, they feel fat. But the difference between them and their bulimic and overeating sisters is this: They don't view their behavior as abnormal, whereas most bulimics/purgers and compulsive overeaters feel horrendous guilt and shame that they can't control their desire to binge, that they secretly engage in purging behavior they uniformly believe is abnormal, and that they can't stick to their resolutions to stop. The bulimics and compulsive overeaters live in a daily nightmare, not at all unlike that of any addiction. And they suffer alone and silent, desperately afraid to let anyone find out the awful truth about them, and unable to stop the behavior without some outside help.

Seeking to understand why she does what she does is your second step on the road to freeing your loved one from an eating disorder. But don't stop here. Continue to search, to read, to ask questions of a counselor or therapist to help further refine your understanding. Only through understanding can you begin to help. In the next chapters, I'll show you step by step how to proceed.

Chapter Three

Look, Listen, and Feel— How to Recognize an Eating Disorder

Sounding the Bottom for Danger

My house sits on a ridge overlooking the Arkansas River in Little Rock. In the winter when the trees are bare, I can sit and watch the river traffic from my windows: barges meandering downstream to the lock and dam below and the tugs chugging upstream, pushing other barges. The Arkansas flows at navigable levels all the way to where it dumps into the Mississippi down in the southeastern corner of the state, thus providing a commercial waterway for the barges that pass below my windows.

Rivers are mutable things, constantly changing, the sandbars shifting with the currents, with floods, with storms, so that even an experienced river pilot will run aground unless he sounds the bottom. In the old days, that meant throwing weighted lines, knotted at intervals, into the river ahead to check the depth of the water. Today, the sounding is done by electronic sonar equipment, but the principle is the same.

Human emotions, like rivers, are subject to change at a

moment's notice. Behavior that seems to be relatively stable or at least "not too worrisome" today—and here, of course, I am referring to disordered eating—may erupt in a torrent of symptoms or escalate dramatically with changes in stress. Living with a disordered eater can be a nightmare for family and friends, too. The emotional ups and downs that the anorectic, bulimic, or compulsive overeater feels will be mirrored in highs, lows, anger, frustration, and worry in those people who must live with them. If you think someone you love suffers from disordered eating behavior—and obviously you at least have your suspicions since you're reading this book—you may have wondered if there are signs to look for that could confirm your suspicions. And the answer is, yes. Once confirmed, are there important tip-offs that might warn you of impending trouble? In other words, can you sound the bottom to see if your loved one is developing a serious eating disorder or running into danger? Yes, again. Let me show you how.

Key Tip-offs for Family and Friends

We've all got our little quirks, strange habits, peculiar ways of doing things, and we consider them to be normal. Other people's quirkiness we sometimes find odd, unreasonable, unfathomable, but still it could be "normal." And so, before you begin to read this section, I insert a note of caution: Please don't pick out one physical or behavioral sign that you may recognize in your loved one (or in yourself) from among all these I will give you, point to it, and say "See, I *told* you she was anorectic!" What you're looking for here is a preponderance of evidence, a pattern of symptoms, not an isolated quirk. A single habit or trait that seems to fit the picture typical of an eating disorder should perhaps heighten your level of awareness and make you take a closer look, but it should not alarm you if it is the only such habit or trait you observe. With that caution, let's dive in. In the anorectic, look for . . .

Changes in her mood or behavior

1. *Perfectionism*—She may begin to manifest obsessive neatness in clothing, grooming, and possessions, or she may feel that she can never complete a project to her full satisfaction. She may suddenly seem to think that no grade short of 100% is good enough, that no amount of study time is sufficient.

Behavioral tip-offs: Adhering to rigid exercise or study regimens, arranging things—i.e., books, records, clothing, even canned foods—alphabetically, by size, by color, by something.

2. *Insecurity*—The anorectic may feel she is not capable of achieving success despite obvious talents and achievements. She may begin to feel that family and friends neither love nor respect her, no matter how often they tell her or show her their love.

Behavioral tip-offs: Inability to accept a compliment with a simple "thank you," self-disparagement, needing constant reassurance or outward and visible manifestations of love or caring.

3. *Preoccupation with weight and food*—The anorectic usually measures her worth by what she has or has not eaten, by how many ounces up or down her weight has shifted, or by how thin she perceives herself at that moment. She may relate to you an intense fear of becoming fat or a fear of food, or you may notice unusual or ritualistic habits related to food.

Behavioral tip-offs: Finding excuses to avoid food-centered social gatherings, hiding food at meals (slipping it into a napkin for later disposal), hiding sometimes large quantities of food around the house, cutting food into tiny pieces, counting bites, rearranging food on her plate, weighing herself multiple times a day, cooking but not joining the family in eating, severely restricting intake or outright fasting. Paradoxically, she may also keep large quantities of the things she forbids herself to eat—cookies and candy are typical examples—in the drawers of her room or in her purse or coat pockets. Maintaining her restrictive vow in close proximity to temptation often imbues an anorectic with a greater sense of personal power.

4. **Withdrawal from family or friends**—Because she feels alone and apart, she may seek to physically as well as emotionally separate herself from those people who "don't understand" the significance or importance of her behavior.

Behavioral tip-offs: Eating apart from the rest of the family— recall that Lindsey (introduced in Chapter 1) pretended to eat in her room while studying. Dressing in layers to hide the truth about her weight loss, staying in her room most of the time, no longer calling or accepting calls from her friends, breaking off a relationship with a boyfriend, preferring to study or work alone, moving into solitary living quarters, and generally avoiding all social interaction when she can.

Note!! You should view increasing withdrawal from the company of friends and family as a major warning sign of worsening anorexia. If you see this kind of behavior in your loved one, take steps today to find a qualified eating disorders counselor, therapist, or physician and make an appointment to speak with them as soon as possible. As in depression—a mood disorder with which anorexia and bulimia are strongly associated—withdrawal from society can presage increasing feelings of worthlessness and despondence, which can lead to self-destructive episodes, and even suicide attempts. Do not ignore the symptom of increasing withdrawal; although in an individual case it may not have anything to do with disordered eating, it is almost always a sign of impending psychological trouble. Seek help.

Changes in her body

1. Profound **weight loss** over a short period of time.

2. **Dizziness** or fainting spells, brought about by low blood pressure, dehydration, low blood sugar, or anemia.

3. **Confused thinking** or uncoordination, consequences of low blood sugar, low blood pressure, or ketonemia (high levels of ketone bodies in the blood that occur with metabolic breakdown of muscle and fat for fuel).

4. *Menstrual irregularities* or cessation of menstruation altogether from protein and fat malnourishment, which brings about a shortage of the dietary precursors—primarily cholesterol—necessary for the production of adequate amounts of reproductive hormones. A condition of metabolic slowdown mediated through the thyroid hormone system may also figure in her menstrual difficulties. Eventually, all anorectic women will lose their menstrual cycling completely.

5. *Pallor*—again, usually from anemia.

6. Complaints of *being cold* all the time. Low blood pressure, low levels of steroid hormones (again from protein/fat malnutrition), and deranged thyroid hormone balance may all play roles in cold intolerance in the anorectic.

7. Development of lanugo (down-soft body hair)—The growth of lanugo, which resembles peach fuzz, probably occurs in response to the low levels of female reproductive hormones (from the nutritional deficiencies), which creates a relative abundance of the male reproductive hormone, testosterone, which all females produce small amounts of.

8. Complaints of *stomachache, bloating*, uncomfortable fullness. This symptom puzzles me, since the anorexic stomach is usually far from full. Most likely, these complaints represent somatization symptoms. You may be more familiar with the term *psychosomatic complaints.* Her mind, rigidly certain that she is fat and that the three bites of a bagel she allowed herself was overdoing, may concoct physical symptoms to validate what she believes or fears.

In the bulimic, look for . . .

these changes in her mood or behavior

1. **Volatile emotions**—Her mood, perhaps normally reasonably stable, may begin to take wide swings from being sad or depressed to feeling guilty (usually about succumbing once again to bingeing and purging), which brings on bouts of self-hatred.

Behavioral tip-offs: Listen for personally critical comments, such as "I don't know why I ever tried to . . . [you name it: diet, run for office, get him to notice me, stop bingeing]." You get the picture. Then followed with, "I know better than to think that I could have done it!" Listen, too, for increased comments about blame, specifically about her being to blame for everything under the sun.

2. **Insecurity**—Like the anorectic, the bulimic places a high value on how much she weighs. Her sense of herself, her personal value, and what she perceives as her worth to others correlate closely with whether or not she believes that she got every last ounce back off of the foods she's binged on lately. She desperately needs and wants approval, but will be suspicious of it.

Behavioral tip-off: You might say, "Ellen, you look just great!" Her response might be to immediately wonder, "What does he mean? Was there something wrong with the way I looked before? I must have *really* been fat before!"

3. **Development of other impulsive behaviors**—Although these associations are not exclusive to bulimics, they, more than any other group of disordered eaters, may suffer other kinds of addictive behavior: gambling, alcohol, pills, or even kleptomania (compulsive stealing, both in the form of shoplifting and taking things that belong to other people.) The kleptomania often involves theft of food, candy, laxatives, but occasionally clothing or other items.[1]

4. **Preoccupation with weight and food**—As she begins to restrict, the bulimic may begin to obsess more and more about the food she feels is forbidden.

Behavioral tip-offs: Conversations with her will begin to revolve more and more around food and her weight. It may be difficult for you to get her to talk for long about anything else.

She may also begin to avoid situations where she knows food or meals are planned, such as social and family gatherings, or dining out with friends. This avoidance may seem odd to you when her disorder drives her to consume big quantities of food, but think again. Her bingeing is her terrible secret, one she doesn't want anyone else to find out, so the voracious eating usually can't be done in public. And she's probably also afraid that if she gives in and does eat, she won't be able to stop herself, and then the truth will be out. Like the anorectic, she would prefer to avoid social eating, but for very different reasons.

5. *Compulsive exercising*—She may run five or even ten or more miles every day. She may do two or three hours of aerobic dancing. She may do both of these. And she may exercise at odd hours. Often, the stimulus to work out is from guilt and self-deprecation over having succumbed to "too much food." Too much may be a true high-calorie binge or it may be a single bite more than she's promised herself she'd eat. She may exercise and weigh and exercise and reweigh until she's satisfied that she worked all the "extra" off.

6. *Binge eating*—Although she will usually begin to hide her bingeing—particularly once she begins to engage in purging behavior—you may stumble in (as Bill did on Ellen in Chapter 1) to interrupt a binge. Witnessing her rapid consumption of large volumes of food should send up red warning flags for you, even if she attempts to explain it away. And even if you buy the story, or allow her to believe that you do, at least keep your eyes and ears open for other signs of disordered eating. But let me add a note of caution here. Beyond simple, straightforward, nonthreatening statements on your part, the moment of your initial discovery of her binge-eating behavior is not the best time to confront the issue. For example, upon his discovery, it would have been most unwise for Bill to have chased Ellen down the hall to the bathroom, pounded on the door, and demanded that she come out and explain herself and her behavior that instant. In fact, at no time should the confrontation occur in an angry or forceful way. Later, when we develop some ground rules for intervening, I'll

delve more deeply into what to do and not to do. But now, let's move on.

Changes you may see in her activities and surroundings

1. *Missing food*—As her secretive eating escalates, food will begin to vanish. You may not—and probably won't—at first see any evidence in the form of wrappers, empty boxes, dirty dishes, because she will work very hard to hide what she's doing. Later, as the disorder progresses, she may be less fastidious about hiding her behavior or cleaning up after herself. It goes almost without saying that life with a friend or relative deep in the throes of bingeing and purging is not a picnic. Once the disorder becomes visible, the aftermath of the binge—sinks full of dirty dishes, partly eaten food, kitchen messes from preparation of food, and messes in the bathroom from the purge—place an intolerable burden on the rest of the household. Working toward a more equitable living atmosphere with your loved one will be an important part of helping her through recovery, but we'll get into this aspect more deeply later in the book.

2. The *appearance of purge-related medications*—i.e., prescription diet pills and diuretics (water pills), over-the-counter diet pills, laxatives, or the emetic Ipecac syrup—in the medicine cabinet or bathroom cupboard usually means exactly what it appears to mean—purging. Although she may not recognize it, her inappropriate use of these medicines is fraught with danger. Ipecac syrup, for example, is a product designed to be used to induce vomiting when it's needed (such as when children swallow poisonous or noxious substances). Bulimics use it to force themselves to vomit after binge eating, and chronic use of it can damage the body, most especially the heart. It is this complication that ultimately caused the death of singer Karen Carpenter, who suffered from the combined eating disorder bulimarexia.

3. *Caches or boards of food*—The bulimic, unlike the anorectic, often eats everything she's bought during the binge and is

likely to throw out anything that's left in the aftermath of guilt she suffers for having binged. So you may or may not find stockpiles of food. What you may discover, however, is the repeated purchasing—and hauling home—of the same kinds of high-calorie, high-sugar, high-fat foods: brownies, cookie dough, cupcakes, donuts, bread, sugar-sweetened cereals, ice cream, potato and corn chips, chocolate milk.

4. *Financial woes*—Because some bulimics can binge-eat food costing up to $100 or more a day, may use fifty to two hundred laxatives a day, or in some cases visit four or five restaurants in a single evening, the cost in dollars and cents to maintain their food addiction may leave them woefully unable to pay their bills. Younger women (teens and preteens) may even resort to theft to support their habit.

5. *The smell of vomit in the bathroom*—There is simply no stronger or more telling tip-off than this one. She may try to mask it with perfumed air fresheners, with disinfectant sprays, or with scented candles, but as a physician, I can attest that the odor of vomit is tough to eradicate quickly. If she's purging through vomiting, and doing it very often, she won't be able to disguise the smell easily.

6. *Frequent trips to the bathroom after a meal*—There is a normal, physiologic reflex (called the gastrocolic reflex) that occurs in all humans when food stretches certain sensors in the stomach. The stretch signal stimulates an urge to defecate, and this urge is not abnormal; it occurs in every person. Most of us, however, are able in a social setting to repress that need to relieve ourselves until a later time. When I say a bulimic visits the bathroom just after a meal, it is not this kind of normal urge she is answering. Her response is usually to induce vomiting by some means to "undo" the meal she's given in to eating.

Changes to look for in her body

1. **Weight fluctuations**—Some bulimics can make weight swings of ten, twelve, even fifteen pounds over a period of a few weeks.

2. **Puffy eyes or broken blood vessels around the eyes**—This physical sign betrays the strain of heaving and gagging and retching. The longer she's practiced, however, the less likely she will be to traumatize herself by vomiting. Some bulimics become so adept at inducing vomiting, they no longer require any stimulus greater than leaning over the commode and giving a little heave. Early on, or with dry foods, getting it all to come back up may require so much strain that the loose tissues around the eyes swell with fluid and small blood vessels pop and bleed under the pressure of the heaving.

3. **Swelling in the cheeks**—The parotid gland, which is the major saliva-producing gland, works overtime under the duress of daily vomiting. Over time, it will enlarge and pouch the cheeks out so that they look like a chipmunk's.

4. **Fatigue**—As with the anorectic, fatigue may come from fluid depletion—not from lack of intake, but from excess output. She will suffer dehydration from vomiting, from emptying the bowels with laxatives or enemas, or from excess urination caused by the use of diuretic pills. She may lose potassium, which can compound the feelings of fatigue and weakness, from the diuretics directly, or from the loss of bowel contents from vomiting or diarrhea. She may not adequately absorb vitamins, minerals, and essential fats and protein, and the deficiencies can lead to fatigue from anemia or malnutrition.

5. **Muscle aches and cramping**—Again, the fluid and electrolyte (sodium, potassium) loss from the water pills, enemas, and vomiting can lead to muscle-fiber irritability, causing the muscles to cramp painfully. Depletion of calcium may also contribute to the muscle problems.

6. **Light-headedness, disoriented thinking, fainting**—Like the anorectic, although with wilder swings, a bulimic may

drift into and out of states of dehydration, volatile blood sugar, high levels of ketones during periods of fasting, low blood pressure, and electrolyte imbalances from fluid loss. All of these may contribute to fainting spells and confused thought processes.

7. ***Tooth decay, especially of the front teeth***—This occurs, not as you might at first suspect, from the huge amounts of refined sugar that these young women consume, but rather from the chronic bath in stomach acid that the tooth enamel takes from her vomiting. Although I doubt that the high-sugar diet helps, the amount of acid produced by mouth bacteria from the digestion of sugar against the enamel (a major cause of decay in the rest of us) is a drop in the bucket compared to the stomach acid she brings up in purging. Most bulimics of any duration who purge by vomiting will have either teeth in bad need of work or a mouth full of expensive dental artistry in the form of caps, crowns, and fillings.

8. ***Chronic sore throat or burning in the chest***—These symptoms probably come from the corrosive effect of stomach acid on the lining of the esophagus and throat. Neither of these structures has a tough enough lining to withstand frequent caustic chemical exposure. If your daughter, sister, spouse, or friend has complained of sore throat after sore throat, and the doctor keeps turning up a zero on cultures for causes, certainly it could be a viral infection, but you may want to find some private means of letting the doctor know what you fear. You have to tread very carefully in this regard if your loved one is an adult, because the ethics of doctor-patient confidentiality demand that the physician not discuss her case with anyone without her permission. This restriction does not prevent you quietly getting this piece of information to him, though. By doing so, you may find in that physician a powerful ally in helping to free your loved one. Remember, a bulimic recognizes that her behavior is abnormal and hopes to keep it a secret. But she may not fully recognize the health consequences of what she's doing. If she hears about the dangers from a medical doctor, however, it sometimes packs a bigger punch.

Timing of this kind of meeting with the physician needs some planning, and we'll get into that in a later section. For now, let's move on to examine the warning signs in compulsive overeating.

In the compulsive overeater, look for these behaviors

1. *Being overweight, but eating like a bird*—At least in public, most compulsive overeaters tend to severely restrict what they eat. They take tiny portions and nibble. I can vouch, too, having taken care of a good many of them in the weight and metabolic control clinic that is a part of my practice, that they will give a sacred oath to their physician that attests to their minuscule intake. I have had countless morbidly obese patients tell me: "Doctor, I just don't eat a thing. I can't understand why my weight just keeps going up!" or "I hardly ever eat sweets. And I only eat one small meal at night. Why can't I keep my weight down? I think it's my thyroid." Well, certainly obesity does arise from endocrine disturbances in many patients, and when it does, finding and correcting the disturbance will help restore them to normal. But for a good many overweight patients—the American Anorexia/Bulimia Association estimates as many as 40 percent—obesity may be a consequence of their disordered eating habits. In front of others they do eat like birds, but alone, like Susan in Chapter 1, they devour huge numbers of calories in binges.

2. *Diet hopping*—My husband, whose medical practice is limited solely to the treatment of obesity and related metabolic disorders, has helped literally thousands of overweight people lose weight and learn how to control their disordered metabolisms to better maintain a healthy weight appropriate for them. In cases of obesity that arise from endocrine (metabolic or glandular) causes, the patients lose weight steadily and do well. The vast majority of these patients have either never tried to lose weight before or have tried only a time or two. Sometimes, however, a patient will confide in him, "I've tried every diet known to man and then some, and none of them work! Can you help me?" When he gets this kind of story, my husband knows that a reordered

eating program alone is not going to be enough. Chances are that this patient will need counseling to help her come to grips with an inappropriate focus on food as a coping mechanism, and he will recommend this kind of therapy as well.

An eating program is not magic; it's merely a tool to help correct an abnormality more quickly. When patients leapfrog from one "diet" to the next, it's usually because they didn't lose weight, and that's usually because they didn't stick to the program. The patient feels that the "diet" failed, and on to the next one. The failure, however, is that someone failed to recognize that in a compulsive overeater, the overpowering urge to eat is not a lack of willpower, it's a physiologic, perhaps biologic, and certainly psychologic addiction. Like the bulimic purger, the overeater uses food like a drug to numb pain, to soothe, to control anxiety.

Restrictive dieting in a compulsive overeater usually only sets her up for a binge and a confirmation of her failure to control her problem—a major negative reinforcer. Complete therapy for a compulsive overeater—or any disordered eater—should include nutritional counseling and the development of healthier eating patterns. However, she most likely knows what she *should* be eating already; she just can't overcome, without some help, her addiction to the feeling she gets from bingeing on the foods she shouldn't be eating. Unless she learns appropriate tools to use in coping with life stress, anxiety, loneliness, she won't be able to wrest herself free of her eating addiction. And no weight-loss tool will do that job.

3. *Avoiding recreational activities*—When weight begins to climb, the compulsive overeater may give up certain activities that she formerly enjoyed out of embarrassment. For example, swimming, biking, boating, golf, jogging, dancing, tennis—i.e., any activity that requires skimpy attire or lots of movement. Recall from my story about Deena that her mother hardly left the house, and that when she did, it was in head-to-toe coverage. This kind of social restriction leads to a greater sense of isolation and loneliness, which only makes the problem worse, depresses her more, and drives her binge behavior. She may come to look upon

food as her only means of enjoyment; she may even verbalize this feeling in defense of her compulsion to eat.

4. *Success and failure ascribed to weight*—The compulsive overeater, especially if she has become obese, tends to blame personal failures (both career and in relationships) on her weight and to credit others' successes to their thinness. Recall Susan's comment in Chapter 1 that the promotions always go to the young, pretty, thin women, not to someone like herself. Although there are usually many other factors upon which success or failure hinges, there may be some basis for this perception beyond a compulsive overeater's psychological paranoia. Many recent studies have shown that there indeed may be some degree of discriminatory bias against the obese both socially and professionally. While obesity may make the road to success more difficult, it doesn't block it entirely. Still, the overeater may erroneously feel that if the weight fairy could just flutter by and bop her on the head with a magic wand and make her thin, then with that instant thinness would come instant happiness, success, romance, and worth. It doesn't work that way, of course, but most overeaters engage in just this kind of fantasy, thinking about what it would be like if only . . .

In contradistinction to anorectics and bulimics, who feel their personal worth tied to their thinness, obese overeaters generally feel their *lack* of worth or intrinsic value is a consequence of their heaviness. The basic value distortion involving weight and worth is the same; the overeaters just come at it from the other direction.

5. *Mood fluctuates with weight gain and loss*—The compulsive overeater may swing from elated one day—usually the day she's discovered the magic new diet that is going to fix everything—to dismally despondent if she fails to lose weight on the diet of the moment or breaks her vow and binges on "forbidden" foods.

Changes in her body may include

1. **Weight fluctuations**—but with a relentless upward trend—The compulsive overeater often achieves short-term weight drops—sometimes substantial amounts—from time to time. But cycles of restriction usually only serve to spark cycles of bingeing, and the binge quickly replaces the lost weight and usually adds on a few more pounds. One step forward and two steps back.

2. **Hypertension** (high blood pressure)—Usually the blood pressure elevations are not dramatic at first—a typical mildly hypertensive reading would be 160/100—but are enough to signal a problem. The elevation of pressure may come about from fluid retention (worsened by high-carbohydrate, high-calorie, high-refined-sugar binges) or may be a sign of early metabolic malfunction, escalating total body fat, and most particularly increasing deposits of fat tissue around the vital organs.

3. **Fatigue**—This symptom can occur for various reasons, many of which arise from nutritional deficiencies. Malnourishment may seem quite odd in someone who overeats, but simply eating large amounts of the wrong kinds of food offers no better source of essential nutrients than not eating enough. Typical binge foods are ones high in refined sugar and mostly devoid of nutritional value, and in the periods between bingeing, she may be trying to adhere to stringent or radical diets that are also nutritionally deficient. So it should come as no surprise that compulsive overeaters—even morbidly obese ones—suffer from deficiencies of protein, vitamins, essential dietary fats, and minerals. From these can come such medical problems as anemia, muscle weakness and cramping, and chronic infections, any of which can bring on fatigue. And finally, as I mentioned earlier, overeaters may also suffer from depression of mood, which can also contribute to a sense of exhaustion.

Is Your Loved One in Jeopardy?

If you have seen behavioral changes in your loved one that have made you fearful—or convinced—that she is eating-disordered, how worried should you become? How quickly should you act? The answer is: it depends. While the development of any true eating disorder in someone you love should prompt you to seek help, anorexia, bulimia, and overeating occur across a spectrum of severity. I've listed below some clues to help you differentiate the worrisome from the dangerous. If your loved one displays any of these danger signs, you should get help for her right away—in some cases, immediately.

1. **Suicidal talk or gestures**—It should go without saying that talk of having suicidal thoughts should be considered an emergency. For any eating-disordered person—but particularly with bulimics, who tend to act on impulse—any mention of "life's just not being worth the hassle" or "nothing to live for," or any gestures, such as toying with knives or razor blades or pills, should never be taken lightly or ignored. Behavior of this kind should prompt you to take immediate action. If there is a psychiatric hospital, a mental health facility, a therapist you have already chosen, even a hospital emergency room, take her gently by the hand and go there. She may not want to go along, but you must try to explain to her why you're concerned and what you intend to do to try to help her.

In some cases, the disordered eater may attempt to manipulate those around her through talk of suicide, but I urge you not to try to differentiate the two on your own. Take any talk of suicide seriously and allow a professional to make the call.

2. **Collapsing or fainting**—Especially in anorectics and bulimics, passing out or becoming too weak to walk unassisted can be an ominous and important warning sign. The causes can range from severe dehydration to heart-rhythm disturbances or even heart failure. If your loved one should collapse or pass out, take her immediately to the nearest hospital emergency room and tell the physician that you suspect (or know) she is eating-disordered. If you have grounds to suspect any other pertinent information—i.e., that she abuses laxatives, enemas, diet pills, or emetics (like syrup of Ipecac)—be certain to give the physician caring for her this information as well. The better informed a

physician is about a patient's history, the faster he or she can get to the root of the problem.

3. *Increasing social withdrawal*—I have already discussed withdrawal as a warning sign, but I include it again here to underscore its importance. As depression gives way to despondence, or as the addictive behavior begins to consume more and more of her waking time, the disordered eater will withdraw more fully into a world that focuses on her obsession with food. Social withdrawal is usually a sign of worsening depression no matter what the cause, and because it may precede emotional collapse and attempts at suicide, you should take it very seriously.

Although not all-inclusive, this list should give you some idea of the major signs and symptoms you should be on the lookout for. So look at her, listen to her. She may be crying out for your help in the only ways she can—through her behavior. Open your eyes and ears and take note of what she's trying to tell you.

Try to put yourself into her place, to feel what she feels about her life, her abnormal relationship with eating. Search your inner feelings; examine your own coping mechanisms. When life gets tough for you, what do you do? How do you cope? Search your heart and wring out of it every ounce of compassion and understanding that you possess. You may need all of it to free her, because the road to freedom from this addiction is fraught with frustration, with obstacles, and with worry. But the payoff at the end of the road you will travel with her will be to see her emerge emotionally stronger, better able to cope with the curves life is sure to throw, physically sound, and recovering. Let me take you now to the road ahead.

Chapter Four

Helping Your Loved One Help Herself

When you set off down the road that leads to your loved one's freedom from her self-destructive behavior, you will need some directions: a road map, a guidebook, an arrow pointing the way. Dorothy, when she set off from Munchkinland, had instructions only to "follow the yellow brick road" to get to Oz. But sometimes, you will remember, she came to a junction in the road where the yellow bricks seemed to go in two or three directions. How was she supposed to know which way to go?

So it will be in your journey toward your loved one's freedom. There is much work for you both ahead, and sometimes it may seem that it all needs to be done at once. To keep you headed down the road in the right direction, I've listed ten Steps Toward Freedom below. You should be able to keep coming back to this list to reorient yourself if you stray from the road for a bit. And I must warn you, some of the tasks will overlap, so you may have to work on several of them simultaneously. And some of them will require your commitment for a lifetime. Let me underscore once again that overcoming dysfunctional and disordered behavior from any cause—or helping someone else in their efforts to do so—requires tireless and total effort at times. Although I doubt you would do so, don't delude yourself that the journey to freedom will be easy. You may sometimes feel overwhelmed by the enormity of the task you've set for yourself, and you may even occasionally feel you should never have undertaken it. Feelings of self-doubt on your part may be magnified if your loved one resists your efforts. You may at times feel that this is a battle you're going to lose, but keep trying; her freedom from the disorder and your freedom from anguish and worry hang in the balance. Every journey begins with the first step, and now is the time to begin.

Ten Steps Toward Freedom for Your Loved One

Step 1

Become informed

I have already given you this assignment (in Chapter 1 when we discussed meeting the enemy), and I hope you have begun already. Let me stress it by saying again that before you can hope to help, you've got to know what you're up against. Otherwise, you will just flail about, willy-nilly, battling an unidentified enemy. And such a course not only gives the enemy the upper hand, it is doomed to fail. To conquer the enemy, you must know it; to know the enemy, you must understand it. Notice I said *understand,* not *agree with.* There's a difference. You cannot agree with what your loved one is doing to herself. Your feelings on that subject more likely run toward bafflement, worry, anger, even resentment. You might naturally harbor some feelings of anger and resentment toward anyone who hurt your loved one—and that includes your loved one herself. You will need to air these feelings later, but please don't feel embarrassed or even guilty for having them. They are not only common, but in many senses, natural.

So no, you cannot agree with or condone her behavior, but you can strive to understand it. Know it from the inside out; learn all you can about the biological, psychological, and sociocultural reasons for her disorder. Read every book you can get your hands on. Turn to the back of this one, and you will find an extensive list

of suggested books, most of which you can get through your local
library or through interlibrary loan programs.

Step 2
Contact a qualified professional for help

The next step on the road to becoming informed and readying
yourself for the task ahead is to make your initial contact with a
psychiatrist, psychologist, licensed social worker, or physician
who has experience (and success) in dealing with eating-
disordered patients. This step, too, I have mentioned before, and
you may have already begun to look for such a person within your
community or through one of the national referral groups I
mentioned in Chapter 1.

Once you have located a qualified licensed counselor or therapist, make an appointment for yourself. The best approach at
first would be for you to meet with this person one-on-one, although if the disordered eater is your child (even a fairly grown-
up one) both you and your spouse may want to go. In Chapter 1,
when I first mentioned the importance of finding qualified help,
I also gave you a list of important questions to bring up at this
initial meeting. You may want to refresh your memory about
those points before your interview with the counselor. But in
addition to finding out more about your loved one's disorder and
its severity and about the next steps to take in bringing her to
professional help, you will want to satisfy yourself that this counselor is someone you, your loved one, and your family can trust.

As a layperson, you may feel you are not in a position to make
such a judgment, and perhaps from the standpoint of assessing
technical abilities that is true. But you will be able to read your
own "gut" reaction to the counselor. By this I mean do you like his
or her style? Is there a good chemistry between you? Do you pick
up a sense of openness, of honesty, of caring, and of ap-
proachability? Do you feel reasonably at ease (allowing for the
discomfiture inherent in discussing an uneasy subject) during
the interview? Do you feel a general sense of confidence, trust,

and belief in what this person tells you? All of these qualities are subtle and vague, but critically important for you to accept and profit from this association. And assessing them requires no special skills beyond your own antennae. From a treatment standpoint, however, let me give you a few considerations that will help you in your assessment.

1. Be sure the therapist is licensed in his or her profession. The exact nature of the license will depend upon what kind of professional you have chosen.

A *psychiatrist* will be licensed as an M.D., a medical doctor, and therefore able to prescribe medications, if needed, and to assess her general state of physical as well as mental health. A psychiatrist will also usually be either board certified or eligible for board certification by the American Board of Psychiatrists, which requires completion of a three-year (or longer) additional training program in the area of psychiatry, after earning the standard general medical degree.

A *clinical psychologist* will usually be a Ph.D., a doctor of philosophy, who has taken a bachelor's degree in college, often a master's degree in a related field, and written a doctoral thesis (requiring usually one to three years) in the field of psychology before being awarded this advanced academic title. The clinical psychologist is trained to evaluate, diagnose, and treat conditions of psychological or mental health without the use of drugs. Should drug therapy become necessary, the psychologist would enlist the services of a general medical doctor or psychiatrist to evaluate and prescribe medications or to assess and treat physical health problems.

A *licensed social worker*, or LCSW, is a trained and certified counselor. To obtain this certification, he or she will have received a bachelor's degree in college (often in psychology, but not necessarily), followed by a master's degree program in social work and counseling, and then will have met the state's requirements beyond that level for licensure. This certification qualifies the social worker to engage in individual, group, and family counseling.

The LCSW is not a medical doctor and like the psychologist will enlist the assistance of a physician or psychiatrist to prescribe medications and evaluate or treat associated medical problems.

The number of years of training to reach certification does not necessarily equate with how adept a professional counselor becomes. You will find excellent therapists, highly expert in working with eating-disordered patients, in each of these categories. By the same token, however, certification and licensure in any of them does not guarantee expertise or facility in handling this particular group of disorders.

2. Ask the therapist for his or her credentials relating specifically to eating disorders and their treatment.

Ask how long the therapist has been involved in treating eating disorders and how many patients (roughly) he or she has evaluated or treated for these conditions. Is this therapist affiliated with a local or regional treatment center that cares for or even specializes in treating eating disorders? Such an affiliation is not a must, but it is a plus. Along these same lines, a therapist with a practice strictly limited to treating *only* eating disorders is not necessary, especially in smaller communities in which a counselor will have to accept clients with a wide variety of problems to keep the doors of the practice open. In larger communities and metropolitan areas, you would be more likely to find a therapist who works exclusively with eating-disordered clients.

3. What approach does this therapist take in treating eating disorders?

The therapist should view eating disorders as addictive disorders—much like alcoholism, drug addiction, or gambling addiction—through which the sufferer attempts to cope with deeper, internal emotional disturbances. Ideally, the treatment should focus on the abnormal eating behavior as well as the hidden stresses or emotions that stimulate it. And the therapist should be willing to educate and guide your loved one toward a clearer understanding of what motivates her behavior and work to help her learn appropriate, new, healthy coping tools to replace the disordered behavior. No compassionate or qualified therapist will view these problems as a lack of willpower. If this seems to be the case, find another therapist.

4. What about family counseling or treatment of the emotional problems of other family members?

The therapist should be willing to evaluate and either treat other family members or make appropriate referral for their treatment. In some situations, it is good for the same therapist to treat more than one family member—at least in a group setting, as in family therapy. In other cases, sharing a therapist can be counter-productive to making progress in sorting out the emotional debris in a disordered family unit on an individual level. In such cases, the ethical therapist would refer additional members to other qualified counselors. Find out how the therapist you've chosen feels about this possibility.

In addition, let me list a few general questions you probably need to address at this first meeting to make matters run more smoothly. Although these issues are nothing more than commonsense questions that arise in any professional interview situation, in the stress of the moment, more than one patient or client has forgotten to ask them. So let me take a moment to remind you to ask:

1. What is the policy on payment? Sometimes the initial visit is even given free of charge. You should ask if this is their policy. If not, is payment expected at the time of service or will bills be sent? What about insurance coverage? Will the therapist accept it as payment? Many insurance companies do reimburse at least a portion of the cost of outpatient mental health services, and the counselor may either file the information necessary to collect the benefits as partial payment, or may require you to pay for the services in full at the time of the visit and let the insurance company reimburse you to the extent that your policy allows.

Sometimes, reimbursement by insurance requires that the counselor meet certain requirements to qualify for payment. Be sure to check with the benefits representative of your own insurance company to see what these requirements may be and what restrictions, if any, apply to mental health services.

2. Do you pay for missed appointments? In general, in the field of mental health, most professionals do charge a fee (sometimes the entire fee for a session) if you fail to appear for your scheduled appointment without giving at least twenty-four hours' notification.

3. What is the cost of their services? Most therapists will charge for their outpatient services by the hour. And the cost for their time will generally depend on the kind of service provided—i.e., individual sessions will be higher than group sessions. Also, practitioners in a private practice setting will *usually*, although certainly not always, be more expensive than in a hospital clinic or mental health facility. Find out in advance what these charges will be.

4. Will the therapist be available to answer your questions about the care of your loved one? Some therapists have a policy of minimal contact and minimal information once therapy has begun. Often there are important reasons he or she chooses not to discuss the patient with other family members—even if the patient is a minor child. Find out at the outset what the ground rules are in this regard, to avoid bad feelings or mistrust and anger later on.

5. If the therapist is not a physician, who will be responsible for medical emergencies, hospitalization, and prescription of medications? Also, who will be responsible for your loved one's general medical care?

6. Ask the therapist to enumerate for you specific crisis situations that should prompt your contact with him or her immediately.

7. How do you get in contact with the therapist in the event of such an emergency? Write the number down and put it in a safe place. Also, ask if the therapist takes calls for his or her own patients exclusively or if there will be times that someone else will be responsible. If others will be involved, who will they be? Call sharing is not unusual, but it's comforting to know in advance what the arrangements are if you should need emergency help at night or on weekends, when the office will probably be closed.

8. Is the therapist affiliated with a particular hospital or mental health facility to which you should take your loved one in the event of crisis?

Once you have made and kept your initial appointment, you will have taken a major step toward freeing your loved one. Next, you must look into your own heart and into the family situation. There may be some housekeeping of your own that needs attention.

Step 3

Conduct a personal and family inventory to identify behaviors that contribute to or promote your loved one's disorder

Your loved one doesn't exist in a vacuum, but rather as an integral part of a sphere of friends, family, co-workers, and classmates. You may be keenly aware of the impact that her disordered behavior has had on you and others around her, but you may have failed to appreciate the extent to which your behavior—as friend, family member, parent, or spouse—affects her and your relationship with her.

In order to be of the most help to her, you will need to take stock of your own problems or those you see in family and friends close to her. The process of self-examination is difficult and quite often painful, but you must commit yourself to this task before your loved one can be free. Be totally honest with yourself—and with the therapist or counselor—in making this appraisal.

For example, if you are her parent, look closely at how you typically interact with your daughter, and at her position in the hierarchy of the family. Would you say you have encouraged her to feel appropriately self-reliant without placing too much responsibility on her? Development of self-worth begins in childhood as a reflection of the worth or confidence placed in us at home by our parents or other significant adult role models. If you impart the feeling to her that she's not capable, she will doubt her capability. Although most parents never intend for their child to feel this way, they can sometimes inadvertently "teach" the wrong message by trying to do too much for their children. By trying to make things easy for them, parents may mistakenly transmit a message that's received as "you're not big enough, strong enough, smart enough, clever enough, pretty enough . . . [pick the adjective] . . . to do this, that, or the other thing."

Or are you perhaps overly protective of her? Again, and usually out of love, parents may create an atmosphere of interdependence of the child on the family unit that hampers the normal spreading of the wings with a transfer of allegiance to a peer group.

Or could it be that you are too dependent on her? Have you placed her in the position of being your confidante? Especially in situations of abnormal family dynamics—divorce, separation, infidelity, alcoholism, or abuse—one parent may turn to a child for emotional support or comfort. These kinds of adult life situations place an emotional load on a child or teenager far greater than her as-yet-immature coping skills can handle. Out of this kind of stress, abnormal coping mechanisms—such as an eating disorder—can arise.

The hardest reality of all that some families must come to grips with is one of family dysfunction because of alcoholism, drug addiction, or abuse. These problems occur with much higher frequency in the families of bulimic young women, but may certainly occur in the families of anorectics or compulsive over-eaters, as well. Family dysfunction may or may not contribute to your loved one's disorder, but I ask that you remember that where it does exist, there is no shame in making that admission; owning up to our frailties, to our failures, to our mistakes is the first, the most difficult—and therefore most laudable—step toward correcting them. There is no shame or stigma attached to admitting these problems that could equal the tragedy of allowing them to continue to disrupt the family by keeping them under wraps. If you feel a problem of this nature is at work in your own family, in your own life, facing it will not be comfortable or easy, and I urge you not to attempt to do it alone. If alcohol or drugs are a part of the problem, a place to begin might be a local chapter of Alcoholics or Narcotics Anonymous, Al-Anon, or Alateen. In addition, you should speak as forthrightly as you possibly can about these problems with the therapist you have chosen to help your loved one. Dealing with your own problems, or with problems within the family, can do nothing but help your disordered eater by creating a healthier climate for her to heal in.

This task begins with your careful inventory of your life, your family unit, and your relationship with your disordered eater, and will not truly end until you have dealt with and dismantled any promoting behaviors you have uncovered with the help of the therapist and community resources. That kind of healing will take your commitment for the long haul, but now is the time to begin the work.

Step 4

Prepare to act by doing your homework: Plan to meet resistance before you approach

The time has now come to meet the problem head-on, to speak with your loved one about what you suspect. Proceed at this point under the specific directions of the professional counselor you have chosen to help you. Discuss these specific points thoroughly with the counselor beforehand:

- When is the best time to approach her?
- What is the best strategy for bringing the problem to light? For

example, should both parents or more than one concerned friend be present? If so, decide ahead of time who will do the talking and perhaps even rehearse with the therapist what you intend to say.
• How can you best identify and dispel your loved one's defense mechanisms? At this point, you may never have even heard the term, so let me digress for just a moment to talk about them.

Defense Mechanisms

You can think of defense mechanisms as emotional armor that the mind constructs and dons to shield it from hurt. These tricks of the mind serve a useful purpose normally, allowing us to carry on through the grief that comes from loss of a loved one or the hurt that comes with disappointments in love or work. But sometimes, the layers of protection we wrap around the psyche can block recognition of the extent or severity of our own problems or those of someone we care for. When this happens, they may block the road to healing, or in this case, the road to freedom from an eating disorder.

The psychological protection a disordered eater builds is no different from yours; she may even rely on this psychological armor more heavily than most. Here are four defense mechanisms you may encounter blocking your progress with her. You will have more success in your initial discussion with her if you know ahead of time what to expect.

1. *Rationalizing*—developing reasons or excuses for the behavior. For example, when Bill first broached his concerns about Ellen's bingeing and purging, she might respond with: "Oh, don't worry. I've only done that once or twice, and that's just because I was so stressed over that big deadline coming up. It just keeps my stomach in knots. Just as soon as I finish this project, I'll be fine."

2. *Denying*—refusing to recognize the problem even in the face of proof that it exists. For example, if Lindsey's weight

continued to decline and her worried parents then discovered the trash bag of uneaten food, a discussion in which she used denial to shield herself from the truth might go something like this:

MOM: "Honey, you've been getting so thin that your father and I are worried about your not eating."

LINDSEY: "I'm not getting thin at all, so no need to worry, Mom. There's no problem with what I eat; I eat a big dinner every night."

MOM: "Well, that's a part of why we're worried. I found this trash bag with last night's dinner in it under your desk when I vacuumed your room today."

LINDSEY: "I don't know what that is, but I didn't put it there. I don't know what you're talking about. I eat every night."

3. _**Minimizing**_—attempting to make big problems seem insignificant and therefore unimportant. When Lindsey's mother, trash bag in hand, tells her of her concerns, instead of denying knowing anything about it and denying that she has an eating disorder, Lindsey might instead say: "Oh, _that_. Yeah, I meant to take that out this morning, Mom. I'm sorry. I just wasn't hungry at dinner, and then I got so wrapped up in studying for chemistry that everything got cold. I just dumped it into that bag so I wouldn't have to look at it. It's nothing, really. I'm sorry I left a mess for you."

4. _**Externalizing**_—blaming people, forces, factors outside oneself for the disordered behavior. Let me show you an example of such a defensive mind trick in Susan's eating behavior. Recall from Chapter 1 that she had failed to get a promotion at work and that the job had been given to another employee. Susan responded by going on a carbohydrate binge, starting with twenty-four powdered-sugar donuts and finishing with the Mexican feast, which most likely consisted of two orders of nachos, a large fruit punch or two, a double enchilada plate with extra beans and

rice, and four sopaipillas with honey. In justifying this behavior to herself—and probably to anyone else who questioned it—she might say: "Hey, the only reason I did that was because I was so upset about not getting that job. I deserved a little treat to a night out to cheer me up. If the people at work would just give me a break once in a while, I'd never have done that." Translation? It's all *their* fault that I ate 6,000-plus calories.

When you speak with your loved one, you will almost certainly see these defense mechanisms in action. Learning to recognize them is only a part of the job; preparing yourself to counter them takes some work. I urge you to discuss how to best deal with each of these kinds of psychological excuses when you speak with the counselor. Then you will be better armed both to anticipate them and to sidestep them.

Step 5

Approach your loved one, under the guidance of the therapist

Now that you've talked with the counselor and you both feel that the time has come to speak with your loved one about your fears, how do you go about it? Let me show you.

1. First, think about the timing. There may not ever be a "perfect" time or place, but try to select a time with as few stresses and distractions for you both as possible. If you're dealing with your daughter who lives at home, pick a quiet evening or an unhurried weekend morning. If it's possible to do so, especially if you're dealing with a teenager, unplug the telephone. The last thing you'd want is the ill-timed ringing of the phone. If there are other siblings, make arrangements for them to be at a friend's or relative's house to circumvent distraction from that front.

If the person is your spouse or a roommate, again, choose a quiet moment to talk when the two of you can be alone. Try to get everyone else—in-laws, children, siblings, other roommates—out of the house to give you some privacy. And again, unplug the telephone if possible.

If your concerns are about a friend, sibling, or other family member that you do not live with, the best course of action would probably be to invite them to your home, since you will be able to control that environment better, thus improving your odds for limited interruption. You could also choose a neutral meeting area—for example, a walk in a local park may give you privacy and quiet.

2. Next, if more than just you and your loved one will be present, think carefully about who should do the talking. Except in the case of parents and children—when often both parents should talk with their daughter—it's probably advisable on the first encounter for only one person to be present. An exception to the both-parents rule would obviously be if there were any grounds to believe that one of the parents might be a contributing cause to the behavior—such as in cases of emotional, verbal, physical, or sexual abuse.

In deciding who will be present, remember that a disordered eater, especially a bulimic, views her eating behavior as both terrible and shameful. She may never have discussed this situation with another living soul, and bringing such a secret to light before a group would only heighten her sense of shame and anguish—even if you're reasonably sure she is aware at some level that you suspect the problem. Being aware that someone knows something and talking about it aloud differ enormously.

3. Decide what you hope to achieve before you begin. Although your heartfelt desire is most likely to _make her stop the behavior_, you must recognize right now that you can't. Only she herself can do that job. Neither you nor anyone else can _make_ her stop the disordered eating, and trying to do so will only compound the problem. Short of that, what do you hope for from this meeting?

If her health has become a concern, you might hope to persuade her to go to a treatment center or to see a physician, or at the very least to speak with a professional about the problem. Reasonably, you might hope to let her know you're worried, that you care, and to let her know that the door is open for a dialogue between you about your concerns and about her behavior. You may also reasonably hope to make a change in how her behavior affects you by bringing it out into the open for discussion. This tack allows you to establish some ground rules—especially if you live in the same household with her—to minimize the impact of her behavior on you and others around her. Whatever your goals, decide before you speak what you hope to accomplish by talking with her.

4. How do you put a voice to your fears? As strange as it may seem to do so, take a pencil and paper and actually write down what it is you want to say. I'm not advocating that you read from a script, but many people can write their feelings better than they can verbalize them. The added bonus here is that you can revise what you've written, but once words leave your lips, they cannot be recalled. It is wise to at least think through, and preferably write out and even rehearse, what you plan to say before you actually do so. You may even want to practice what you want to say with the therapist who is helping you.

However you go about preparing what you will say, when you actually begin the dialogue you must remain calm in the face of any behavior she may respond with. Don't respond in kind. Just keep calmly telling her that you're not judging her or her behavior, you're only concerned for her and want to help. Her reactions could include:

Anger: *Mind your own business! Stay out of my private life! Leave me alone!* Such a response is not an uncommon one when you're bringing up a touchy subject, particularly one she would just as soon keep hidden. Try to remember that she's like a startled kitten, surprised and perhaps feeling embarrassed or violated by the revelation you've just made. And like a frightened animal, she's bristling and reacting with offensive hostility. Stay calm. Continue to say: "I don't want to violate your privacy, but I can't help being concerned, because I love you. I have to let you know that I'm concerned and why."

Indignation: *How dare you?! How could you spy on me like that?! Who do you think you are, accusing me of this?!* In reacting in this way, she tries to enlist guilt as her ally. She's trying to make you feel as though you've persecuted her wrongly and maybe you'll feel so rotten that you'll just forget the whole thing and go away. Come back to her with calmness: "I'm not accusing you; I'm worried about you because I've heard you vomiting at night in the bathroom, or I found you like that on the kitchen floor, or I found the trash bag full of uneaten food in your room. These things concern me because I love you. Because I love you, I want to help if I can."

Projection: *Who are you to talk about my behavior? You drink booze like a fish. You're not perfect either!* Here, she's trying to turn the tables. Of course you're not perfect. No one is perfect. But she's trying to use your own flaws to make you doubt the correctness of your being in any position to speak to her. Again, maybe you'll feel so overwhelmed by your own problems that you'll forget all about her and hers. Don't buy into this behavior. Come back with: "I know I've got problems, but right now I want to talk about what I fear is happening to you because I love you. Later on, we can deal with mine, too, but right now your behavior is what's concerning me, because I saw the three empty cartons of ice cream in the trash this morning and I'm worried about you."

Disbelief or denial: *I'm amazed that you would think this! There's no problem. I'm fine. You're mistaken.* Although any disordered eater may deny her problem at first, the anorectic is especially likely to do so. Remember, she usually does not feel that her behavior is abnormal or disordered. She may go to great lengths in her efforts to persuade you that you're wrong. You should always be aware of the possibility that such might indeed be the case; you could be wrong. The strength of your convictions will depend largely on what you have seen and heard, and any other solid information you've obtained about eating disorders. If you have repeatedly overheard her vomiting or smelled the vomit in the bathroom, that's pretty solid evidence and you shouldn't give in to self-doubt too easily. If you've awakened on several occasions to find that everything to eat in the kitchen has mysteriously vanished overnight and only the two of you were there, again, that's firm enough grounds for your concern. If you can see a steady decline in her weight, her clothing hanging on her, hours and hours spent exercising, at least these give you pause to inquire. Tread carefully on information you've gotten second- or thirdhand, or on a single episode of abnormal behavior. You may need more ammunition than recycled tales to stand your ground with her.

Although I would encourage you not to be put off by her initial denials and give up too easily, you also don't want to badger her and belabor your point. To do so would be to risk creating a negative atmosphere in which she would become even more defensive and secretive. Under such circumstances, your best option may prove to be a tactful retreat to regroup; just don't allow yourself to be dissuaded too easily. You must walk a fine line here, and it's not easy to know when to stay pat or when to fold. Your chosen counselor may be able to give you some guidelines about how far or how hard to push this initial meeting. Just tell her in as calm, forthright, and frank a way as you are able exactly what you fear, why you fear it, and what you'd like to see happen. Don't sidestep the issue with vague allusions to what you fear; put a name to it. For example, Bill should say to Ellen: "Honey, I'm concerned about you. This is very hard for me to say, but since I found you in front of the refrigerator the other night and then heard you in the bathroom vomiting, I've been worried that you are a bulimic. I'm afraid of what this could do to you, to your health, and to us, because I love you. I want to help if you'll let me." Like Bill, you should speak your mind gently, but plainly, calling the behaviors what they are and voicing the rational reasons for your worries. If she still will not or cannot admit the behavior, leave the door open for her, and tell her you want to try to talk about it again at a future time.

Relief: *I'm glad it's over. I'm glad you know.* Bulimics, in particular, feel a sense of relief once their secret is out in the open. And it's not hard to see why that would be if you put yourself in her shoes. Have you ever, in childhood or even in adulthood, said or done something or found out information that you feared to tell anyone else about? Or something that you hoped no one would discover? Most of us have, and if that's true for you, too, think back to that time. Recall what a heavy burden that secret knowledge placed on your heart and mind. The weight of the secret pulled you down, didn't it? Your mind anguished over the possibilities: What if someone finds out? Then everyone will hate me, or no one will trust me, or they'll all laugh at me, or I'll get into serious trouble for this. Worry over what your mind could conjure up in the event of discovery consumed you. And then, when the secret finally did come out, and the consequences weren't nearly as dire as you had feared, you felt lighter than air, like you could float with that horrible weight lifted from your heart. So it often is with the disordered eater. Although I don't want to lead you into a false sense of hope that most initial talks end up on so satisfying a note, the flood-of-relief response is indeed possible. She may indeed greet your discovery with, if not a flood, at least with some sense of relief. And if that should be the outcome from your initial meeting with her, count your blessings and get her into therapy.

Step 6

Formal intervention

In some cases, your private discussions with your loved one may prove fruitless. She may stubbornly refuse to acknowledge that she needs help even in the face of worsening problems. If you are a parent dealing with a young teenager, you most likely do have some degree of leverage to firmly insist that she has to speak with a professional about the problem, but her acceptance of the need certainly helps grease the skids toward recovery. But when the anorectic, bulimic, or overeater is an adult, short of her being in a life-threatening situation, you can ask, suggest, plead, and bargain, but in the final analysis, you cannot force her into therapy. So, what then? With the help of your counselor, you can *intervene* on her behalf. In many cases, what you could not accomplish one-on-one, a group of concerned friends and family can. The technique of formal intervention has worked time and again over the years to bring inveterate practitioners of other addictive and destructive behaviors—drinking, drug use, gambling—to treatment, and it may be the approach that will help your disordered eater begin to find her way to freedom. How do you go about this group approach?

1. Begin only with the guidance of the counselor you've chosen.

2. Select a group of four to six family members and friends that she knows well, loves, and respects who will form the intervention team. Prospects for the team might be her spouse; her child or children (if mature enough to participate) or her own siblings; her parents or grandparents; her priest, rabbi, or pastor; a close friend or co-worker; her personal physician; a favorite teacher or professor; a coach or athletic trainer. What the team members must have in common is a concern for her, a desire to help, and the ability to stay calm during the meeting. They needn't be professionals in intervention. If they love and care about her, if they've seen the deterioration, if her behavior has had some sort of impact on them, they can help.

One word of warning, however, no matter how strong any individual's desire to help her may be: You should exclude anyone from the team—and this includes spouses and parents—who cannot keep a lid on anger, whom she does not trust or fears, or anyone who has a known addictive problem of his/her own. For example, to include even a parent who has a known problem with alcohol or drugs (and perhaps has yet to admit this problem) is to invite her to turn both barrels onto that team member and place the whole team into a defensive scramble. So, choose the team with care; the success of the attempt hangs in the balance. Now is not the time for ego-salving of people who express a sincere desire to help but whose presence might hurt the effort.

3. Each team member should spend some time thinking about and then writing down his or her recollections of specific instances regarding her and her eating disorder. Include times when she has left the bathroom or kitchen in a mess, when she has

ravaged the shelves of other people's food, or when she has perhaps even stolen money or food. Recall episodes in which the behavior has interfered with her social life, her career, her financial security, or her relationship to you or others. List any concrete physical or health-related symptoms, such as fainting spells, heart problems, high blood pressure, difficulty concentrating, tooth erosion. Each team member should try to be as specific and precise in creating this list as possible, right down to dates and times if you can. You will each use this information during the intervention meeting to help her realize on the one hand that those who love her know the extent of her problem, and on the other, that her behavior has had a damaging and hurtful impact on people she loves. Stick to the facts, because truthful specifics will hit home, whereas vague euphemisms can leave her room for emotional escape. Completing this task will be difficult and could even be painful, but your reward for these efforts will be resolution and healing. Don't be afraid to write down and say the truth, no matter what that truth is. Bringing your knowledge out into the open will help to free her.

4. Rehearse the intervention as a group under the guidance of the counselor until the whole team feels comfortable with what's to be said. Every team member who intends to be present at the actual meeting should be available to go through the preintervention rehearsal, so that you can act in concert, not inadvertently lay down verbal or emotional mine fields for other team members to skirt. The team should designate one member as the captain. It will be this person's responsibility to be certain that the group stays focused and to be the spokesman for the group as a unit.

Although you cannot know with certainty ahead of time what her responses will actually be, with the counselor (who ideally has been through this before with others) you can anticipate what she will be likely to do and say, and in rehearsal the team can formulate a cohesive response to as many defensive maneuvers as possible.

5. As with your private one-on-one talk, the team needs to settle on clear goals for success in the intervention. At this stage of

the game, however, the stakes are usually higher, and the hopes and expectations of intervention usually include her accepting some form of treatment. The severity of her symptoms will naturally dictate the extent of treatment that the team seeks. For example, if she is still functioning at work or at school and her health is not in acute decline, persuading her to enter an outpatient treatment program and perhaps become involved in a community self-help organization (like Overeaters Anonymous or a local chapter of ANAD) would be a realistic goal. If, however, she has withdrawn socially, developed serious health problems, has ceased to function at school and work, or is in financial or legal trouble, these circumstances demand a more vigorous treatment program, such as admission to an inpatient facility. With the help of the counselor, develop a clear idea of what you hope the intervention will achieve before you begin.

6. Be prepared to bring whatever influence or leverage to bear during intervention *and afterward* that you must. Decide who among you has the most leverage with her and the greatest degree of influence on her behavior. Someone she respects—be it a friend, a grandparent, a teacher, a physician—and who she truly believes is impartial or has her best interests in mind will hold enormous sway over her actions. This person (or these people) will influence her behavior. She will trust and believe them, and their presence on the team will go far toward encouraging her acceptance of treatment. That person may or may not have any degree of leverage over her, however. Leverage implies actual consequences that an intervening team member could bring to bear on her should she refuse to recognize the problem and commit to trying to solve it. The appropriate use of leverage can be a potent force in furthering the team's goal. But what's leverage?

An example of leverage might be that her boss, who has discovered she's taken money from petty cash to support her eating, would be willing to simply let her replace the missing money—and avoid facing prosecution—if she will enter treatment. Or perhaps she has been charged with shoplifting or petty theft of food, and again the charges could be dropped or reduced if she would commit to a treatment program. Or it might be a parent who has enabled her to continue the eating disorder by picking up hot checks or bailing her out of debt or paying her rent when she spends every dime on food. The leverage would hinge on going into treatment or losing the support.

Ideally, there will be no need to use leverage at all, since the team members may be able to persuade her through their influence alone. Let me point out here, however, that when the team resorts to leverage, they must still give her a choice: She can do as they ask and accept treatment, or she can continue in her behavior and suffer the consequences. The choice is hers to make, but the team then must be willing to see the consequences through. Nothing would transmit a more garbled message to her than to threaten consequences that she fails to suffer in spite of her refusal to get help.

Under the combined weight of the group, acting as one, she will have a harder time minimizing, denying, externalizing, and rationalizing the effect of her actions.

7. With the help of the counselor you have chosen, arrange for her admission into the outpatient or inpatient treatment program beforehand. Have everything ready so that on the day of intervention, the team is prepared to take her there immediately. To delay getting her to the help she needs—even for a day or two—might jeopardize the success of the intervention by giving her time to work up a sense of remorse over having made the commitment and to back out. The adage "strike while the iron is hot" never fit a situation so well.

8. Where should the intervention occur? Preferably in neutral territory, in a quiet space that would make her hasty departure difficult or awkward. But it could be any place, from a relative's home, to a picnic pavilion in a quiet park, to a hotel room, to her own home.

9. Go forward! Once you've selected the team, determined your goals, rehearsed completely, and chosen a place and time, you're ready to intervene. Let me take you through the intervention that Bill arranged to persuade Ellen that she needed help

after his private discussions with her failed to bring her to treatment.

The intervention team consisted of Ellen's mother, one of her brothers (Jim), the pastor (Reverend Simms) from the church she and Bill attended, her gynecologist (Dr. Caswell), her secretary (Martha), and Bill. The group had completed all their preliminary tasks, written out and rehearsed their dialogue again and again, and finally felt they were ready. The intervention site and time this group chose was Ellen's office after everyone else had gone home. Bill had told her he would meet her there for a late dinner in the city.

> BILL: "Ellen? Hi, hon. I brought a couple of other people along."
>
> ELLEN: "Oh, really?" She looked up to see her secretary, Martha, standing behind Bill. "Haven't you left yet, either, Martha? I thought you had a meeting tonight."
>
> MARTHA: "I do, Ellen. That's why I stayed."
>
> ELLEN: "What's going on here?"

The rest of the team walked into her office together and quietly closed the door.

> ELLEN: "Mom? Jim? Reverend Simms? Dr. Caswell? What is this? Bill, why are they all here?"
>
> BILL: "Honey, we're here to help you. Each and every one of us has come here tonight because we care. We love you and we're worried about you."
>
> ELLEN: "Oh, for crying out loud! I don't have time for this! Is this some kind of a joke?"
>
> DR. CASWELL: "No joke, Ellen. I came out here tonight because I'm concerned for you. Do you remember when you first became my patient? It was only a few years ago; you came because your periods had become irregular. It didn't seem like too

bad a problem at first. But remember just a couple of months ago, you came to me again because you hadn't had a period in three months, and you were afraid you might be pregnant, but after I examined you, we talked about the possibility that you might be bulimic. You said I was crazy—"

ELLEN: (interrupts the doctor) "Why are you telling everybody this? This is my private business, not theirs. You're not supposed to tell other people about me."

Jim, Reverend Simms, Bill, and Ellen's mother all jumped in together to defend against Ellen's attack on Dr. Caswell. It is critical that the team function as a cohesive unit and that they close ranks to prevent the disordered eater from engaging in divide-and-conquer tactics. It would be much easier for Ellen to excuse/rationalize/defend/deny her bulimia against an individual than a group.

JIM: "No, you're wrong, Ellen. If you think we all already didn't know what was going on with you, you're off the mark."

MOM: "Jim's right, dear. You even told me yourself you thought you might be pregnant then. Dr. Caswell is trying to help you."

REV. SIMMS: "We're here to help you, Ellen, not to cast blame on Dr. Caswell or anyone else. We've all come to talk to you, to let you know we're concerned about you, so please just listen to what we have to say. Martha, why don't you go next."

ELLEN: "Next? What are you all going to gang up on me?"

MARTHA: "We care about you, Ellen. I've been worried about you for months, since you've been having those dizzy spells. Then, last week, you fainted right here in the office when you leaned over my desk. You hit your head so hard that if this carpet weren't so thick, I'm sure it would have done more than just make a big knot."

ELLEN: "I don't see the big deal, Martha. Have you never gotten dizzy and blacked out? Everybody does once in a while."

MARTHA: "Wait, I'm not finished. I've also been in the ladies' room when you've come in after having lunch meetings. You didn't know I was there, but I knew it was you in the stall heaving. I recognized your navy pumps. I think you may have an eating problem, Ellen, and I'm frightened for you, because I care about you."

ELLEN: "Great. I appreciate your caring, but I can handle my own problems. You tend to yours."

JIM: "Sis, if you could handle this alone, it wouldn't be getting worse. I'm ashamed to say I've suspected something was wrong for years. Really since before I left for college. We shared a house—and a bathroom—remember. And I used to hear you, creaking down the stairs late at night, when Dad had been on one of his tears knocking Joe and me around. I'd lie awake in the dark and wait. In an hour or two, I'd hear you in there in the bathroom, puking your guts up. I was too dumb or young, or too . . . I don't know what, to understand what was going on then. I guess I just figured you were upset about Dad's tirades and his drinking."

ELLEN: "Jim, that was years ago; it doesn't have anything to do with now. Dad's Dad. That part of our lives is over. What can I say?"

JIM: "Let me finish, sis, because I don't think it's over. Last month, when we all got together at Joe's for Thanksgiving dinner, I went into the bathroom after you'd been in there. Ellen, it smelled like puke. You'd sprayed some of that powder room spray in there and burned a match and all, but it still smelled like puke. Ellen, I think you have an eating disorder. I'm afraid this vomiting business is becoming dangerous for you now, and because I love you, I can't watch you hurt like this anymore. I'm asking you to get some help. We all are here to help you."

Each member of the intervention team gave Ellen his story of how her eating disorder had affected her and them and their lives. Bill spoke last.

BILL: "Honey, I love you, but I'm scared for us. For you. For the family we want to have someday. Now that I look back, I guess I've let my involvement in my own career blind me to what's been happening with you. I've heard you vomit in the bathroom before. Like when the firm was deciding on who would get a full partnership, you vomited nearly every night then. You said it was just nerves, and I let myself believe that. But when I found you there in the kitchen last month, well, I guess I couldn't ignore this problem anymore. That's when I knew you were in trouble. I had managed to ignore the fact that our grocery bill is about triple what two people ought to spend on food in a month, but that and the fact that you hardly ever eat a whole meal when we're together should have told me something. But it didn't, and I'm sorry. But, honey, I agree with Jim, and Martha, and Dr. Caswell and the rest. I think you have bulimia, and I think you need some professional help to stop doing this to yourself. I love you too much and value our future together too highly to keep quiet about this."

REV. SIMMS: "Ellen, we want to help if you'll let us. We have spoken with a therapist who deals with eating disorders, like your bulimia, and she has agreed to talk with you tonight. Just to talk. Just the two of you. She can help, Ellen. Won't you come with us now to see her? You don't have to commit to anything more than just this first step, just to talk with her."

All the team members then reassured Ellen of their desire to help, to go with her to see the counselor. Against the combined force of their love and caring, and with what she had believed to be her secret behavior brought out into the light, Ellen's resolve that "she could handle this" crumbled. She was finally able to admit her bulimic history and to accept their offer of help. This intervention proved successful in getting Ellen into treatment.

I don't want to give you the impression that all interventions run this smoothly or culminate so quickly in success, but properly planned and orchestrated, many do. Typically in an hour or less, the team approach will soften the resolve of the most addicted bulimic or compulsive overeater. Anorexia may prove more difficult, but I would urge you not to give up too easily. Even in the face of what appears to be stalwart refusal to admit the problem, or commit to seeking help, success can hinge on the group's persistence and resolve.

If, after every team member has spoken and perhaps respoken, your loved one flatly refuses help, still all is not lost. At this point, however, you may wish to end this session and plan to try again at a later time. Don't become visibly frustrated or angry about her refusal, and don't appear to throw your hands up in the air and give up. Doing so would send her a negative message. Be clear with her that the door to help remains open and that when she's ready to come through that door, you will all be there ready to help her.

If you've used any leveraging methods to attempt to persuade her, and she has chosen not to comply with the need for professional help, be fully prepared to carry out your promise. Absolutely do not let her "off the hook" for any reason. She must face the consequences of her decisions or else the group may as well have announced at the outset: "We're not serious about this. And so you don't really have to do what we ask, because we won't do anything about it anyway!" Not the message your intervention was designed, planned, rehearsed, and carried out to send, is it?

10. Once you've succeeded in getting your loved one to admit her problem, get her professional help as soon as possible. Preferably immediately. Just as Bill and the intervention team did for Ellen, have access to the treatment you've chosen ready and waiting. The biggest hurdle is behind you once your loved one agrees to help. Don't let poor planning at this point undermine your reaching your ultimate goal. Then, once you've placed her into professional hands, let your loved one and her counselor dictate the extent of your involvement from that point on.

Step 7

Set reasonable goals for the pace of progress

It's tempting, sometimes, to feel that once a disordered eater is in therapy, the problems are over, and in some sense that's true. At least the secrets are out and the work of healing can begin. But the operative word in that sentence is work. She's got a load of work ahead of her to overcome her disorder and to learn to cope with the social or psychological forces that got her there to start with. And she may not be alone in having work to be done. If other family members and friends have emotional or addictive problems of their own that have contributed to her disorder, they must begin to address them as well.

It's also not unusual for there to be a kind of co-dependency between the disordered eater and the family and friends who have lived with her, supported her financially, and often unwittingly enabled her dysfunctional behavior. If you think such a dependency exists for other family members, friends, or even perhaps for yourself, examine the possibility closely. Could there be any sort of gain—albeit an unhealthy one from an emotional standpoint—for anyone else from the effects of her eating disorder? At first blush, everyone would likely answer, "No, absolutely not." But refer back to your task to conduct a searching moral inventory. Sometimes we martyr ourselves to someone else's problem—be it alcoholism, drug addiction, physical disability, or in this case, disordered eating behavior—to avoid dealing with our own. An agoraphobic mother (neurotically phobic about social interaction) finds a convenient excuse to never leave home if she must care for a sick family member. An alcoholic father can seek refuge from coming to grips with his own dysfunctional means of coping if he rationalizes that his daughter's bulimia keeps him so overwrought and concerned that he *has to* do something to calm his nerves. Is your loved one's disordered eating behavior providing any gain for friends or family by excusing them from personal responsibility for their own dysfunction? Facing this kind of possibility is painful, but critical to the family's mental and emotional normalization. Take stock now and try to honestly confront dysfunctions where you find them with the help of your counselor or through community self-help organization.

Remember, too, that your loved one has been attempting to cope with the forces that stress her—whatever they are—through the eating disorder. I would be remiss if I neglected to note that the removal of this means of coping—even though it is an abnormal and unhealthy one—is very like removing a bandage from an infected wound: it's painful but important to tear it away, and once that's done, a raw, weeping, angry surface still remains that must heal. Life with her in the first days and weeks after she has abandoned this tool she's relied on to cope with her anger, frustration, fear, stress, or sorrow but before she's learned new, healthy coping tools can be horrible. Be prepared for wild swings of mood, for volatile emotions, for hostility, and all of the other torrent of emotions she's blunted or covered up through use of her eating disorder.

Let's take a look at what can happen when a disordered eater must confront stress without relying on her abnormal coping mechanism (of disordered eating behavior). Let's take as our example Susan, the young woman with binge-eating disorder (or compulsive overeating), whom you met in Chapter 1. Recall that Susan had lost out on a promotion at work and had attempted to cope with that stress through a powdered-sugar-donut binge with a Mexican feast as a chaser. What might have been the result had she not stopped at the store for the donuts? Let's see.

Susan left work hurt, disappointed, and angry about not getting the new job. She walked out to her car, her head spinning with negative, distorted thoughts.

SUSAN: (*Aloud to herself.*) "How could you be so stupid? You should know better than to have even tried for that job. The boss hates me; everybody knows that. Probably because I'm fat. He's probably going to fire me and replace me with someone thinner.

By the time she drove into the driveway and parked, the irrational and negative thinking really had her in its grip. When her husband met her at the door, her raw emotions exploded in his face.

GEORGE: Hi, honey. How'd it go today?

SUSAN: (*Slamming down her purse on the kitchen counter.*) Why'd you park the truck so far over in the drive? I couldn't even get by it to pull in and I could barely get the door open far enough to get out. And then I pulled a run in my new panty hose trying to squeeze by. So thanks to your thoughtlessness, I'll have to go back to the mall tonight to get a new pair!

GEORGE: I'm sorry, hon. I didn't think the truck would block you out. I . . .

SUSAN: That's your big problem, isn't it. You didn't think. When do you ever think about anything but yourself? Or your damn football or basketball games on TV? When do you ever think about me?

Without the mood-blunting effect of the donut binge to mask her pain or to allow her to wrap it up and shove it back into a dark corner of her unconscious, Susan's raw emotions—anger, frustration, and the disappointment over her job—boil over in a misdirected fashion at her husband. She's taking him to task for the way he parked the truck, blaming him for the fact that she couldn't get by the car and ran her nylons. But is any of this what really stressed her? Are these inconsequential events what have her in this state? Absolutely not. All the same, the anger has been flung in George's face, and it's now up to him to respond. He can either escalate the anger (a poor choice) by responding in kind—fighting back, accusing, defending his actions—or he can try to lead Susan to a more rational outlook (a better choice) and defuse her rage. The choice he makes at this juncture is critical to their emotional well-being. George must remain calm in the face of her misplaced rage and remember his task to seek to understand before he tries to help. How can he do this? He must try to gently uncover the true source of her anger, the "why" of her action.

In Chapter 1, I told you how the stress of disappointment stimulated Susan to binge, because that was her means—however abnormal—of coping with stress. But what has happened now, without that "tool" for coping? What can she do with the anger, the hurt, and the feelings of disappointment? They're still there, seeking another outlet. And can George do anything other than batten down the hatches to ride out the fury of her emotional storm? Let's see.

Anger, hurt, frustration, and disappointment are normal human emotions. And the events that cause us to feel these emotions are also a normal part of human life. Susan can close her eyes and wish they weren't, but inevitably, there these stressful situations will still be, waiting to be dealt with somehow—in a healthy fashion or an unhealthy one. Neither she nor George can change the external causes of her stress—she didn't get the promotion, someone else did, and that's the truth of the matter. (Although you'll note she has yet to open up and tell George about the job.) But while she can't make the cause go away, Susan can begin to learn healthier ways of coping with the negative or unpleasant feelings that resulted from the disappointment. Where she coped through bingeing in the past, her new task is to learn to sort through the feelings honestly and to begin to express them appropriately. There is little doubt that a part of her rage also stems from the fact that at that precise moment she would probably have liked nothing better than to dive headfirst into a box of two dozen donuts and eat her way to the top. Feeling the urge to return to food as a coping tool will naturally be strong at times of emotional stress, and abstinence from disordered eating compounds the stress level. Susan must learn not only to identify and anticipate the stressors in her life but also to work out a plan of action when she begins to feel the urge to binge to reduce the stress level. She must learn to back away from the moment—to count ten, if you will—and to say aloud, if necessary, "Time out! Reality check! What are you feeling? Answer: I'm angry. I'm hurt. I'm disappointed. OK, I'm a little envious, too. Now, self, *why* are you feeling these things? Answer: I didn't get the job, but I'm quite competent to do it. I'm good at what I do, and I would have liked to have had the challenge the promotion would have given me. And who wouldn't? The hours and money are a little better, too. And I've been with the company longer than Jill, even though she's got a graduate degree and I don't. Hey, it's not the last promotion that will ever come along. If I just keep up the effort, my time will come."

In short, Susan has to take stock of what's true and keep it in perspective, so the stress doesn't overwhelm her. With her therapist's guidance and through her own hard work and commitment, she will begin to find new ways to handle disappointments. I must urge you to remember in dealing with your loved one that neither the changes in outlook nor the acquisition of new coping skills happens overnight. In the first few months of living with a disordered eater who has just begun to confront her behavior, all those around her may have to weather more than a few emotional hurricanes much like the one that hit George when Susan got home. Now let's take a look at his approach.

GEORGE: I'm sorry about the way I parked the truck and about your nylons, but we can fix those things. I'll go back up to the mall with you later, Susan, but what I'm

more concerned about right now is what's really bothering you. I think maybe there's more to it than just
how I parked the truck or a pair of panty hose. Let's
talk about it, honey. I want to help if I can. Did
something happen on the way home from work to
upset you?

SUSAN: (Still enraged and shouting.) No, nothing happened
on the way home! Not that you or anybody else in the
world would care if it had.

GEORGE: (Very calmly, yet directly.) Of course I care. I think
you know me well enough to know that I do. And I
know you well enough to see that you're hurting
about something bigger than panty hose. Won't you
just talk to me? (Silence for what seemed to George
like a week.) Whatever it is, honey, we can face it
together, can't we?

SUSAN: (She has begun to cry softly; big tears well up in her
eyes and course down her cheeks. When she speaks,
George must strain to hear her.) Jill got it.

GEORGE: Jill?

SUSAN: At work.

It takes George a moment to realize that the "why" of Susan's
anger had been the promotion. She'd been passed over for the new
job, and her anger stemmed not from anything he had done, but
from this disappointment at work, with all the riot of feelings—
hurt, rejection, and loss of self-esteem—that attended it.

GEORGE: (Taking Susan into his arms as she cries.) I'm sorry,
honey. I understand how disappointed you must feel.
I know you could have done a great job for them in
the new place, but you know, you're pretty valuable to
the company right where you are now.

Two important things have happened here. First, George
didn't let Susan's rage infect him; he was able to keep his compo-
sure, to remain calm in the face of the fury. (At times, this

response can require the patience of Job.) And second, Susan had responded to the stress, finally at least, by communicating her sorrow honestly instead of coating her feelings with powdered sugar. The rage and hurt and disappointment are still there, the reality of losing the promotion is still there; what's not there is the reliance on a binge to cope with the stress. Susan's not home free—she's still got a lot of work to do in therapy to unlearn unhealthy responses and learn to express her feelings honestly, but she'll get there.

The important point to remember is that the healing process will take time, sometimes many months or years. At first, you may measure success in terms as small as her remaining in therapy as she and her counselor begin to feel their way along the road to her freedom. Entering treatment does not confer on her some sort of magical power that she didn't have before to abstain from her disturbed relationship with food; she may regress into her disordered pattern at times. What must change, however, is the secrecy. She must develop a sense of openness and accountability at least with the counselor, so that she can be up front about regressions. Often, the counselor will ask her to enter into a contractual arrangement under which she promises to tell if she finds herself tempted to slip into her old pattern of coping with food or if she actually gives in to the temptation.

As someone who loves and cares for her, you will naturally want to know how she is doing. She may feel comfortable about your having that knowledge or not. Simply ask her about it. Tell her at the outset that you care, that you're interested to know anything about her therapy and her progress that she feels she wants to tell you. This approach opens the door to discussion, but doesn't seem to pry. Leave it up to her to tell you, and if her choice is not to do so, so be it.

Step 8

Take the eating disorder off center court

If you've been successful in getting your loved one into treatment, congratulations! If your attempts have so far not set her on the road to freedom, don't give up on her. Give her some room now to approach the door you've opened at her own pace. Whether she's finally getting the care she needs or is still resisting treatment, you and others deeply concerned about her must get on with the business of your lives. Dealing with her and her disorder can become the main focus of your life, and you may have unintentionally neglected other important areas: your work, your marriage, other children, your friends. Try now to find the balance you've lost for a time. Strive to reduce the emphasis on her and her problem with food, and give equal time to the rest of your life. Turn the struggle over to her now—after all, she's the only one who can do this job. It's her battle, her life, and under the guidance of the professional you've helped her find, it will be her victory to win. Let her win it. What I'm suggesting will be difficult for you; I recognize that. But the next step is to let go of the emotional tangle of her eating disorder and to regain equilibrium in your own life. Both for her sake and for yours, you must do this.

In helping you to return to equilibrium, let me recommend two excellent books: Stephen Covey's 7 *Habits of Highly Effective People* (Simon & Schuster, 1989) and Michael Glasser's *Take Effective Control of Your Life* (Harper & Row, 1984). These books show you, in a well-written, down-to-earth way, how to step off the psychological and emotional roller coaster that has become your life. The Covey book gives you a means to bring your life back in balance, by encouraging you to schedule time each day to develop yourself and your relationships in all of life's arenas without allowing one problematic area to consume all your time and energy, overshadowing the rest. The Glasser book teaches you how to take control of those things in your life that you realistically should have control over and to learn to relinquish attempts to control those facets that you cannot control. Learning to differentiate what we can and can't control is a difficult, but not impossible, task.

Let me add here that the Glasser book teaches control theory, and until she has recovered more fully, I would not recommend it as reading for your loved one. Restrictive anorectics especially, but all disordered eaters to some degree, live in a desperate state of "overcontrol" most of the time. The problem lies with the tool they use to do the controlling, which is, of course, food. In therapy, your loved one will learn better tools for coping with—or controlling—stress. At that point, the book may prove to be of greater value to her. It will be of great value to you and others who love her now.

Step 9

Recognize your limits

Among those things we cannot control are *other people's actions and behaviors.* You are not and cannot be responsible for your loved one's eating behavior. That's her job. Yours is to support her efforts at healing appropriately and to tend to the building of healthy relationships with her and others. Whether she starves, or binges, or purges, or abstains from these behaviors is not up to you. She has to make those choices day by day.

If you could have solved her eating problems by just wanting it for her, you'd have done so long ago. But you can't. That doesn't mean you can't continue to want it for her, to keep hoping and praying that she will be able to conquer her addiction to disordered eating, to do all you can to support her through therapy. It just means that you don't have any ability to change her behavior. None at all. When you feel frustrated about not being able to *do something,* remember the words of the Serenity Prayer:

> *God, grant me*
>
> *the serenity to accept the things*
> *I cannot change*
>
> *the courage to change*
> *the things I can*
>
> *and the wisdom to know*
> *the difference.*

The wisdom part is the hardest. You will have to work every day to recognize, admit, and accept the limitations of what you can do for her.

Step 10

Continuing to heal the family

While you're at the business of accepting your limitations in helping your loved one recover from disordered eating, you should take stock and recognize your limitless potential to change yourself. Just as she is solely responsible for overcoming her problems, so, then, are you for dealing with your own. Since none of us is flawless or always does the right thing, there is always work to be done. Always room for improvement. I ask that you now look to the future, look ahead ten, twenty, even fifty years. If you could write out a "history in reverse" for yourself and your family, how would you like it to read? What would you like to see happen? Spend considerable time thinking about this—let your imagination go. Within the confines of the reasonably possible, sketch out the finest next few decades you can envision. Now, I'm not talking here about materialism—I don't mean for you to list that you'd like a villa on the southern coast of Italy, a private jet, and three limos, one for your Manhattan apartment, one for your London flat, and one for your beach house in Malibu. I'm talking about envisioning the finest next few decades for the real you— the spiritual you. If you were able to choose, what kind of life would you hope to lead? What kind of relationships would you build? What contributions would you make to improve yourself, your home, your family, your community, the world at large? What would you want other people to think or say about you after you've lived this life? More important, what would you think about yourself?

Now pull away from this larger perspective and come back to the present. Think about what steps you could take—one of them at a time—to begin to work toward building this kind of future. You could start by reestablishing a healthy relationship with your disordered eater as she attempts to recover. You could begin by confronting any behavioral problems of your own that may stand in the way of living the kind of life you've just envisioned. You and other family members could begin with group counseling to expose and heal the rifts from within and to develop healthier mechanisms for responding to stresses from without.

To bring your loved one to therapy, to help her struggle through the recovery process, but to leave in place the psychosocial forces that contributed to the problem would be lunacy. And so the process of family healing must take place. Like her struggle, the struggle to achieve lasting change will be slow. Like her, you and the family will be *always recovering and never recovered.* There will always be work to do to build, protect, and maintain the healthy relationship you hope for with her and with each other.

Chapter Five

Twelve Steps to Your Own Freedom

If you're trying to free someone you love from an eating disorder, what if that someone is yourself? It's not at all uncommon for disordered eaters—especially bulimic purgers and compulsive overeaters—who *want* desperately to quit these behaviors to read a mountain of books about stopping the disorder. There's a chance, then, that some of you reading *this* book are the loved ones to be freed. If that is the case, and you've come this far down the road to seeking help, do it. Do it now. You're not alone in your addiction to food. Millions—and I mean this literally, millions—of other men and women have suffered the same agonies that you do. Many have recovered, and you can, too. All you need is faith and a desire to try. The seeds of success are within you now to stop your disorder; you need only to carefully nurture and cultivate them for them to grow. You cannot and should not try to make your way alone; fortunately, there's no need for you to have to. Help is all around you, if you will just reach out your hand.

Because you're reading this book, you recognize your problem; at least to yourself you've admitted a need to stop the disordered eating behavior. That's a start. I spoke earlier about setting off down the road to recovery as Dorothy did on the way to Oz. Remember that she needed to find her way home, and that her fellow travelers, the Scarecrow, the Tin Man, and the Cowardly Lion, thought they needed brains, a heart, and courage. You, like them, will need all three of these things to find your way home to the healthy place you once knew. Also, remember that when they finally got to Oz, the Wizard told them the powers they sought had always been in them; they just didn't realize it. The same is true for you. Open the door to freedom and let the power to recover flow out.

Concerned friends, family, or strangers who have yet to become your friends are waiting right now to help you find the strength to help yourself. Count me among those strangers who want to help you. Reach out; we're here.

I want to provide you with some arrows to point the way to your freedom. I have adapted a version of the Twelve Step Recovery Program—originally developed by Alcoholics Anonymous and used for so long and with so much success by its members and other fine organizations, such as Narcotics Anonymous and Over-eaters Anonymous—to be your guide along the road. Let me show you the way now, a step at a time.

Step One: *I admit to myself that I am powerless over my addiction to disordered eating and that because of the addiction, my life has become unmanageable.*

Most of you have already begun to take this step by beginning to collect and read books, like this one, about how to recover from your disorder. But what you've recognized in your thoughts, you may never have voiced. I want you to do that now. Alone in your room, but out loud, repeat the words in Step One. Say them several times until their meaning sinks in.

Step Two: *I believe that a Power greater than myself resides within me, and that this Power can restore me to sanity and freedom.*

It doesn't matter what you call that Power within each of us—a divine spark, the Holy Spirit, the spirit of God in humans, or even the Force. By whatever name, it's there, a force or power bigger than any individual person: an untapped capacity to heal, to change, to improve, to cope. What's lacking is your faith that it's there. So begin to build that faith; give voice to the belief. Multiple times each day, repeat the words of Step Two like a creed. I believe . . . I believe.

Step Three: *I turn over the care of my will and my life to this Higher Power (whatever I understand it to be).*

Release the burden of your care into the hands of a Power greater than yourself. Offer up your need for help in controlling your addiction. Know that the Power to free you is there, ready to accept the burden of your disorder, ready to give you the strength to cope moment by moment, bite by bite, day by day.

Step Four: *I will write a searching and fearless moral inventory of myself.*

Be honest with yourself. What do you see when you shine the light of inquiry on your heart, on your mind? The time for hiding, disguising, and game playing is past. Be straight with yourself. I want you to take pen and paper now and begin to enumerate all the behaviors and feelings that seem to drive you to binge, to purge, to starve. Writing down the triggers that have prompted you to engage in disordered eating makes them real, but more important, turns them into concrete things you can deal with. Write down what makes you angry; list whom you get angry with and why; be honest about what frustrates, irritates, or frightens you; make note of what makes you feel sorry for yourself, guilty, or ashamed. What kinds of stress situations have propelled you toward bingeing or starving? What happens at work, at school, at home that you would like to see changed? What changes would you like to see in yourself? Don't worry at this point about whether you have any ability to bring about the changes; just set down on paper what you'd like to see changed if it were possible. Below each item you list, also note how that situation makes you *feel* and what you have done in the past to take away the unhappiness or loneliness or pain. For example, Susan in Chapter 1 suffered a disappointment at work when she was passed over for the promotion. She felt anger, resentment, frustration, self-pity, and in response to these stresses, she lost herself in two dozen powdered-sugar donuts and a major Mexican-food extravaganza. Search yourself. Unflinchingly examine your feelings and responses, and write them down. Remember, only by admitting what you're up against can you hope to fully release the care of that problem to the Higher Power within you.

Step Five: *I admit my problem, not only to myself, but to the God I believe in, and to at least one other living person.*

If you are near a telephone, pick it up. Do it right now. Call a friend and tell them you need their help. Call your parent or sibling and tell them you need their help. Call a co-worker or a pastor and tell them you need their help. Or call the American Anorexia/Bulimia Association at (212) 734-1114 or the National Association of Anorexia Nervosa and Associated Disorders at (708) 831-3438. Pick up the yellow pages and look under Eating Disorders, Professional Counselors, Psychologists, or Crisis Intervention Services. All you have to do is just say the words: "I think I'm bulimic or anorexic or eat compulsively, and I need some help to get well." This concrete step is the most important one in your recovery. Take it.

Step Six: *I am ready to get well. I am ready to turn over my recovery to the Higher Power within me and to let this Power remove the barriers I have erected that have prevented me from recovering.*

At first blush, you probably will see Step Six as blatantly obvious. Of course you're ready to get well; why else would you be reading this book? But take another look. Wanting to do something and being honestly ready to accept the work and pain of doing it really aren't the same thing at all. Take the time you need to come fully to this commitment. Remember, your disordered eating behavior didn't begin yesterday, and it won't end with the snap of a finger. Controlling your stress through food or through unrealistic restraint have become normal to you. You've come to rely on this behavior to cope with the stresses of life, and letting go of the safety net can be scary. But as is true of any leap of faith, you've got to make it wholeheartedly, secure in the knowledge that a Power greater than you can and will strengthen you and lead you out of your dependence on bingeing or purging or restriction. You must be ready to relinquish your control over your addiction (which has not worked) and, in its place, accept on faith that the Power that has worked within so many will work within you, too, if you will give yourself over to it. When you can make the commitment that you're ready to recover, not just from your lips, but from your heart, you've completed Step Six.

Step Seven: I surrender my control and humbly ask the God of my belief to remove my shortcomings.

Again, when you're ready to tackle Step Seven, I would encourage you to give it voice. Don't just *think* a prayer for help, say it strong and loud: "Help me, God. Take away my hardheaded resistance to let go, my wrongheaded thinking that food is an answer, my willful ego that made me think I could control this alone, my false pride that wouldn't let me accept the help of others when it was offered. Take me into your care, just as I am, both the good and the not-so-good of me. Let me humbly accept Your help. Let me learn to love and forgive myself and remain humbly aware that although I am not perfect, I don't have to be. Help me to recognize that I am not alone."

Step Eight: I must identify in writing all the people I may have hurt through my behavior and be willing to make amends to each of them.

Over the years, because of your disordered eating behavior, you may have eaten other people's food, left rooms in a mess, violated their trust, lied to them, said hurtful things to keep them at a distance or to preserve the secret, caused them worry, stolen money or food, isolated yourself from their love, spurned their attempts to help you. Whatever you can think of, whoever you feel you may have hurt or wronged because of your addiction to disturbed eating, put it down in writing now.

Step Nine: I will make things right again. I will seek out everyone hurt by my behavior and repair the damage, unless doing so would harm them or others.

A part of coming face-to-face with the truth, of having no more secrets about your disordered eating, and of getting well is to free yourself from the burden of guilt that indulging in your disordered eating has created. The confession and amendment of each slight, however minor it may seem, will lighten the load and allow you to go forward unfettered, with a clear conscience and a brighter outlook. Your friends and loved ones knew something was wrong; they may have even suspected long ago what the something was. They will welcome your overtures to set things right between you. Only through completion of Step Nine can you start fresh down the road to a new, healthy life.

Step Ten: I understand that my recovery is a continuing process, and I vow to continue it through ongoing self-examination. I will be honest with myself about myself and my behavior, and with the help of the Higher Power, I will admit it promptly when I am wrong.

If you have begun the recovery process by abstinence from your disordered behavior—with the help of a counselor, a community self-help group, or a formal recovery program—you must remember that it takes time and daily commitment to achieve your goal. You must unlearn the abnormal patterns of coping, through bingeing, purging, or restriction, that you have relied on in the past and replace them with newly acquired, healthy mechanisms to handle the stresses of life. Because none of us is perfect, there may be times that you will forget the lessons you are learning, and may be tempted to revert to old habits of coping. There may even be times when you succumb to the temptation; such are the frailties of the human psyche. What you must insist on in yourself, without compromise, is total honesty. No more secrets.

No more defense mechanisms thrown up to hide the truth. None of this: "It was just one little teensy binge and purge. That doesn't really count." If you find yourself tempted or actually do fall into these old patterns of behavior, you must immediately admit what's happening. Admit it not only to yourself, but to those concerned people around you who have helped you so far. Instead of despairing that you'll never get over these urges, use the moments of temptation to refine your understanding of what triggers the urges. Then, the next time you'll be better prepared to cope. Envision the temptations as red signal flags, waving to warn you that you've still got some work left to do in developing other mechanisms of coping with this kind of stress. (See the later section entitled "Coping Strategies" on page 118.) You must learn to think of yourself and your recovery from disordered eating as projects under construction—as they say, "always recovering, never recovered." And you should feel absolutely no shame in making this admission. After all, unless we allow ourselves to stagnate, that's what every one of us should be thinking. As long as we live, we must continually search for ways to improve our lives and the lives of those around us, constantly probing for spiritual, physical, and emotional soft spots that we need to shore up. Stephen Covey put it succinctly in his 7 *Habits of Highly Effective People*, which I recommended earlier: "The only time you can coast is when you're going downhill." Abstinence is work; recovery is work; life is work.

> **Step Eleven**: *I will keep the channels open between my conscious self and the Higher Power working within me. I will pray daily for knowledge of what I must do and for strength to carry out this work to keep recovering.*

What you must not let yourself forget is that you no longer need to try to face your addiction to disordered eating alone. With the help of the God of your understanding, you have already come face-to-face with the truth of your behavior by admitting it to yourself and to other people; you have owned up to the consequences of this behavior to yourself and others; you have begun to make amends to those you have hurt by your behavior; and you have turned control of your life over to something greater than yourself. Through your work in therapy, you will learn that you are an important part of something that connects us all, and that there is a special reason for you to recover: to live a productive and healthy life and contribute to the world in a way that you alone can.

What you have accomplished by the time you reach this step has required many weeks, even months, of soul-wrenching work, and yet the task is only just begun. You must learn to ask for the guidance that the Higher Power within you can give. Every morning when you arise, spend a few minutes opening that channel, tuning in to the strength and organization you can find there. Make this your morning prayer: "Guide my footsteps, point the way. Help me to accomplish those things which I need to do, and to sort out the important from the unimportant. Give me strength to abstain from disordered eating one more day. Remind me when I falter, that in eating or restricting food I will not find help, only confusion. Light my way today from the darkness of this disorder."

Step Twelve: *Let me become a candle to light the way for other disordered eaters out of darkness and into the warm sun that is recovery.*

If you have firmly ensconced yourself on the road to recovery, think back for a moment. What monetary value would you place on your recovery? How much is freedom from disordered eating worth? There is no amount of money that would take the place of regaining your sanity and freedom. You've gained something without price, and now it's time to give something back— something more valuable than money. You must return in kind. Pass along a tiny bit of your success to someone else who is suffering as you once did. Give something back by reaching out your hand to help another anorectic, another bulimic, another compulsive overeater, and show her how to free herself. Share the wealth of love and the connection to the Power that has pulled you through.

Become an activist and advocate. I don't mean to imply that

you must become a community political activist in the fight to save young women from eating disorders, although that is one avenue that you might choose if that suits your temperament. I only mean that each of you can help by remaining active in your group, in local self-help organizations, as a volunteer in a treatment facility, manning a hot line. It really doesn't matter how you choose to serve, only that you serve in whatever way you can. When you give of what you've received, the wealth is not divided, but multiplied.

I remember that I had a poster when I was in college that a friend had given me during a particularly trying time I was going through. It read: "The love in your heart wasn't put there to stay. Love isn't love 'til you give it away." The poster's long gone, lost in too many years, too many moves. But the sentiment stayed with me. It's true for love and it's true for learning. You've got to pass it on. Share your love and your learning with someone who's still struggling in that unhappy place you left. Now someone needs your help. Reach out to them.

Coping Strategies

In therapy, with the help of your counselor, your support group, and your family and friends, you will begin to learn to rely on new and healthier methods of coping with the stresses that are an expected consequence of life. It's no great revelation for me to say that life isn't always pleasant, fun, happy, easy, and nice. As human beings—both in childhood and as adults—we will meet situations or people that cause us to feel hurt, disappointment, anger, resentment, and frustration. We cannot change this reality, but we can learn to handle problems in ways that do not damage us or those around us.

A large part of your therapy with your counselor or in groups will involve learning to rely on these healthier coping skills. It takes time to unlearn destructive methods of coping, such as bingeing, purging, or restricting, and to replace them with a reality-checking strategy that allows you to turn distorted perceptions into truthful ones, negative thoughts into positive ones, and prevents you from wrongly placing blame on others or yourself. One of your first tasks will be to build a strong emotional bulwark that will withstand the gale-force winds that sometimes blow up with emotional storms. Then, protected by that bulwark, before the storm, when your mind is clear and your emotions are on an even keel, you will want to plan ahead for what might come and what you will try to do to ride out the storm. But first you will need a new set of "tools" to replace the disordered methods of coping with them through food or restriction that you have relied on in the past. Let me introduce you to a few techniques of coping that may make your work a little easier. Your start-up supplies for this exercise include a notebook and a pen or pencil.

Batten Down the Hatches: Steps to a Healthier Coping Plan

1. *Make a list of your stressors.* Take some time to think about all the possible situations that could create stress in your life and write each of them at the top of the worksheet pages provided at the back of the book. Make your list as complete as you can. What is it that bothers you? Is it a difficult work situation? A problem in your relationship with your spouse, parents, friends? In the past, what has caused you to feel emotional distress, guilt, frustration, anger, resentment, depression, anxiety, loneliness, or negative thoughts? What situations have caused you to feel the need to cope through binges, purges, or food restriction? List everything you can think of. Your list might include such categories as marital problems; loss of a loved one through death, divorce, or separation; career dissatisfaction; health concerns in yourself or a loved one; lack of emotional support from friends or family; being a perfectionist; unemployment; personal or family abuse situations; controlling spouses or parents; unreasonable expectations of others; obesity; money troubles; school failures; physical disability. Try to be honest with yourself about what upsets you.

2. *Write down how each of these situations makes you feel.* Next, write down what kind of emotion each of them has inspired in

you before. Above all, be honest about what you felt. These notes are for your use only, unless you choose to share them with your counselor or someone else. Don't put window dressing on your feelings to make them more "presentable" or "nicer" for someone else. Make it honest and truthful. If your blood boils when your mother doesn't trust you to repair your own shorts with a safety pin, write that down. "It makes me want to scream, throw things, cry, or curse when Mom treats me like I'm incompetent." If you feel hurt or angry and resentful if your husband calls you "Chubs" or "Thunder Thighs," write down just how it feels.

3. *Describe fully what you usually do, or have done before, to express or communicate those feelings, or what you do to cover them up.* In the next few lines come face-to-face with what your responses to such situations have been in the past. When your husband has been unkind to you and his actions have hurt you or angered you, what did you do to communicate your feelings to him or to deal with the hurt? Did you calmly say to him, "You know, Bill, I understand that you're probably just kidding around and don't intend to hurt me by calling me 'Chubs,' but it really does hurt. I recognize that I am overweight, but I'm working on that. I wish you wouldn't tease me about it." Or did you internalize the pain and hide your hurt from him? Did you brush it off externally while inside you were crushed by the thoughtlessness of his remark? Did you feel sorry for yourself, feel like a failure, or feel a loss of self-esteem? More important, did you numb the sting of your hurt by consuming half a dozen brownies—just for starters? Be totally honest about what you have done in the past to soothe hurt, to calm anxieties or rage, to forget loneliness or loss. Don't try to soft-pedal your responses; it's crucial to lay them out in the open. Remember, you must unmask the enemy before you can defeat it.

4. *Reality Check: What's wrong with this plan?* Write down now, while your head is clear, what you know about the dangers or consequences of your old way of coping. What consequences to your health do you risk from binges on high-calorie, high-sugar, or high-fat foods? What consequences to your health does purging through any means (vomiting, enemas, or exercise to the extreme) carry?

5. _Make a plan of action to use healthier methods to cope with the stressors._ Now comes the work. You may want to get some input from your counselor or from other members of your support group to begin to fill in these next several lines. But in this section, what I want you to fill in is a plan of attack for each stressor. Now, while you're not hurt or angry or disappointed, write out what you would like to do the next time such a situation arises. Let me show you an example:

Step 1. Stressor: _Being left out at parties._

Step 2. Feelings: _I'm hurt. I look at the other girls who are no prettier than I am and yet they have all the guys around them and here I am alone in a corner. I envy them in their tight jeans. I feel lonely even in the crowded room. I want to cry and leave or scream out "Hey! There's somebody else over here." I feel ugly and unlovable._

Step 3. Response: _I withdraw farther into the corner or go into another room and pretend to do something, pretend to be interested in a painting on the wall, pretend it doesn't bother me. Then I leave early to go home, but on the way stop instead at the ice-cream parlor and order a triple-scoop fudge brownie banana surprise with extra whipped cream and nuts. Then I follow that with a bag of chips and cheese dip, and maybe a big glass or two of chocolate milk. I just keep going until I don't feel anymore. It's like it's not me who's eating all this food. Then, maybe, I vomit it all up. And then it doesn't hurt anymore._

Step 4. Reality Check: _When I binged on the ice cream and chips I may have consumed 2,000 relatively empty calories. The strain on my metabolism to deal with that avalanche of food weakens it and makes my blood sugar swing wildly. The overfilling of my stomach confuses its ability to help regulate the quantity I eat. When I purge through vomiting, the stomach acid damages my teeth, my esophagus, and my throat._

Step 5. Plan of Action: _When I am at a party, I will be more outgoing and friendly. Although I am overweight, my weight is not a measure of who I am or how lovable or unlovable I am. Those qualities, like my value as a person, come from within me. I will recognize that I am allowing my own insecurities to push me farther into the corner and to_ *isolate me from happiness. Other heavy girls have friends and fun, and I can, too. Working on restoring my weight to a healthy level is a separate issue that I will begin to deal with.*

Now it's time for you to formulate your own plan of attack, to shore up your coping bulwark, so that when the emotional wind picks up, you'll be ready for it.

Chapter Six

Current Therapies for Disordered Eating

W hen you begin to look at the treatment programs and therapies available to help your loved one recover, you may find yourself comparing this approach to that one and trying to determine what's best. Certainly, the professional counselor you've chosen to assist you will have the best idea of what kind of program would benefit your loved one the most, but you'll be better equipped to understand exactly what it is you're comparing if I've given you some basic information. The most important point to remember is that you're looking for a holistic approach. By that I mean a program that doesn't just focus on one narrow aspect of the disorder, but on the disordered eater as an integrated and whole being: the emotional, the physical, and the interpersonal or social components.

A comprehensive approach to the treatment of an eating disorder should first, of course, direct attention to curbing the disordered eating behavior, but it should also aim to uncover the psychological underpinnings that led to and perpetuated the disorder. Then, ideally, the therapy should assist the disordered eater in building stronger and healthier methods of handling stresses.

On the physical side, the treatment should seek to identify and correct any biological or metabolic disturbances that may be contributing to or that were caused by the disordered eating pattern. For example, bulimics who purge through vomiting will need a full dental evaluation and repair of any damage; bulimics who abuse laxatives or enemas need a more thorough gastrointestinal evaluation than anorectics or compulsive overeaters who do not purge; and all disordered eaters will need sound nutritional reeducation. We'll examine each of these components in its turn, but let's begin with the psychotherapeutic aspects, because here is where the most work toward recovery will generally occur.

Psychotherapy

Eating disorders are clearly psychological illnesses, even though there are without doubt other factors involved—biological, genetic, and sociocultural forces. However, the basic area of dysfunction across the board is in the application of food as a tool to relieve emotional or psychological stress. Comprehensive psychotherapeutic treatment of an eating disorder, therefore, demands that the therapy identify the stressing stimuli, among which could be abnormalities in her family or interpersonal relationships, her abuse of drugs or alcohol, other family members with drug addiction or alcoholism, sexual abuse problems or incest, her own inadequate self-image or distorted body image, or any number of other stresses. It is only by uncovering the demons she's trying to combat using food or restriction as a weapon that a disordered eater can learn adequate, appropriate, and healthy techniques to cope with them.

In many cases, psychotherapy can serve as a tool to root out the stresses themselves and allow for real change in these areas. For example, in the case of Ellen's bulimia, therapy brought her father's history of alcoholism to light as a contributing cause of her eating disorder. One role of family psychotherapy might be to allow him a venue to begin to deal with his addiction and admit/confront the havoc it has wrought on his family. At the very least, Ellen and her brothers and mother could learn through their family or individual therapies and through participation in such community self-help organizations as Al-Anon or Adult

Children of Alcoholics what impact his alcoholism has had on them and how to cope with it in ways other than through disordered eating or other addictive behaviors.

As I have mentioned, the psychotherapeutic setting can take one of three basic forms: individual, group, and family therapy. Let's look now at how each works.

Individual Therapy

In this setting, the disordered eater (or some member of her family) visits one-on-one with the counselor for a *session*, which usually lasts between forty-five minutes and one hour, once or twice (or even more often) a week at first. As the name implies, the focus in this kind of therapy is on the individual, her stresses, her response to them through disordered eating, her associated problems, and on the feelings that underlie her behavior. The initial goal of therapy is to curb the disordered eating and to change her irrational attitudes about food and eating.[1] Not all therapists will approach the problem in this manner, but it is one advocated by many experts in the field of psychotherapy for disordered eating and one that makes the most empiric sense to me. Because the eating disorder usually is only a symptom of the problem and not the problem itself, to engage in a therapy that aims only to stop the behavior and not to probe for why the behavior occurs is like treating a fever with an aspirin and never looking for the strep infection that causes it. I have always advocated that it's best to cure the cause, not just the symptom, of any condition. For disordered eating, curing the cause demands active participation on the part of the anorectic, bulimic, or overeater with her therapist in bringing that root cause to light.

Before a disordered eater can actively participate in her own therapy, however, she will need to be in a mentally alert state. If her thinking is still confused from the effects of starvation or purging, or if she suffers from other addictive behaviors as well, such as alcohol or drug abuse, these conditions should be addressed first. Thus, the importance of a comprehensive approach to her treatment.

Once she's clear of mind and thinking straight, the first aim of therapy will usually be to work on the disordered eating patterns themselves—i.e., using methods to reduce the frequency of binge or binge/purge episodes in the bulimic or overeater, or to increase intake in the restricting anorectic.[2] Most research into the efficacy of psychotherapy has focused on the technique of behavioral therapy; especially in bulimics, cognitive behavioral therapy does seem to clearly reduce binge/purge frequency.[3] The best results of all in bulimics seem to occur through a combination of cognitive behavioral therapy coupled with a second technique called "exposure cue and response prevention." In the former, the bulimic and her therapist undertake a probing analysis aimed at identifying what situations seem to stimulate the eating urge. Why does she respond to the stimulus as she does? What feelings does her response through food engender? What feelings does it blot out? And so on. The latter involves having the client eat typical "binge foods" in front of the therapist and then remain sitting with him or her until the urge to purge has passed. The basis for this kind of therapy is that self-induced vomiting gives the bulimic negative feedback through its capacity to relieve anxiety. If she can become comfortable that the anxiety (heightened by eating binge foods) can and will dissipate with time or through other means, she will begin to believe in her own ability to curb the behavior.

Once there is visible progress in the reordering of her relationship with food, work can begin on uncovering the stressing stimuli, and then finally on helping her to learn better ways to cope with these stresses. The end result of this kind of psychotherapy is both to gain control of or to stop the abnormal eating behavior and to get at the *why* of it. Why does she do it? How did the abuse of eating become a tool for coping? What need is the behavior meeting for her? What other means can she employ to meet that need more appropriately?

Group Therapy

Some feelings of isolation, loneliness, or "differentness" usually accompany disorders of eating behavior, and these feelings serve to further separate the anorectic, bulimic, or compulsive over-eater from the society of friends and family. Therapy done in groups of five or six up to a maximum in most cases of ten to twelve members can provide a crucial link to congenial socialization, as well as offer a safe and comfortable venue for her to openly discuss her eating disorder. Once formed, the group may be ongoing (open-ended) or may have a specified time limitation—i.e., scheduled to meet weekly for six weeks or eight weeks or six months, or whatever.

An exception to the use of a group setting, however, is when the disorder causes withdrawal into the world of the self in the extreme—which is more likely to be the case with a severely restrictive anorectic or a bulimic purger with extreme metabolic derangement from purging. In this instance, group therapy may not be a good idea, at least for a time. At the zenith of her disorder, for example, a seriously disordered anorectic may have so totally blocked out everything except her quest to be thin that she may not be able to interact with the other group members in a way beneficial for her or for them. And, as I mentioned before, severe restriction or purging may have temporarily impaired her ability to think and reason coherently, which in and of itself would not be conducive to successful group interaction. Again, this highlights the need for a comprehensive approach that would identify and correct any metabolic or physical imbalances that would prevent her alertness and cooperation.

For the group to be therapeutic and beneficial, the members must also develop a sense of trust and respect for one another. Without that, they can make little progress together. In some cases, the group members become close enough to be available to support one another in times of crisis or temptation, which is an added benefit for those women who have felt alone and isolated by their disorder. The therapeutic impact of hearing others admit that they, too, have engaged in similar obsessions and compulsions regarding food, eaten in similar ritualistic ways, succumbed to purging through vomiting, enemas, laxatives, or exercises will help to exorcise the ghosts in her head that have whispered "You're different. Normal people don't do this. You're weak. If other people knew, they'd despise you." In breaking through these self-erected myths and fears, she takes a giant step toward freedom from the disorder. The positive connections generated in a well-matched group can be powerful healers.

At our nutritional and metabolic clinic, we enlisted the help of a clinical psychologist to lead a series of time-limited behavior- and insight-oriented groups focusing primarily on learning new life skills to cope with stress that take the place of food-related coping. These groups dealt primarily with compulsive over-eaters, and several of them became in effect ongoing groups, because the mix of people proved so congenial. The group members enjoyed the sessions so much that at the end of their allotted time, they wanted to re-form the group for another go. I don't want to mislead you into the belief that all the groups ran so beneficially; some of them did not. The point is that group therapy offers benefits that individual therapy cannot: friendship, camaraderie, a support network, an arena for exchange of ideas and feelings, and instant feedback from others in the same situation. In conjunction with one-on-one sessions, group work is an important part of comprehensive psychotherapy in disordered eating.

Family Therapy

As its name implies, the "client" in this setting is the family unit, which may be parents and siblings of younger patients, spouses and parents of older patients, or any member of an extended family network who lives in the same house with the disordered eater or has played a major role in her upbringing, or whose own behavior/addictions may have contributed to the stressing stimuli that inspired her need to cope in the first place. When the eating disorder involves an adolescent or teenager, the impact of the family is usually so great that including some form of family therapy would be a sine qua non for a comprehensive approach.

In the family setting, the therapist and all members of the family unit who are to be involved in the therapy usually meet for weekly sessions that last for about one hour. The sessions themselves focus on family interaction, with the disordered eater as the primary concern, but usually extending to include other relationships.

Take, for example, the case of Lindsey, the high-school-aged anorectic you met earlier. Because she is relatively young (about age fifteen), a part of her comprehensive treatment plan included family therapy. During these sessions, Lindsey, her parents (Rita and Tom), and their therapist, a psychologist named Dr. Gibbons, began by discussing what effect Lindsey's eating disorder had on the family as a unit. As is sometimes the case, Lindsey's family did not seem disordered on the surface. Her mother was a very successful trial attorney in their community and her father a busy cardiovascular surgeon. They shared a luxurious home, and Lindsey attended the finest schools and the most exclusive camps in the summer. To Lindsey's recollection she had never heard a cross word spoken by either parent to the other or to her. Outwardly, they seemed more together than the Cleavers or the Nelsons or any other idealized television family ever conceived. Then, one day in family therapy, Dr. Gibbons saw a chink in the armor. Let's see how that chink opened up a giant chasm that Lindsey had been attempting to bridge through starvation.

DR. GIBBONS: "Lindsey, don't you ever get really mad about something? I mean really steamed up about something you think is unfair to you or maybe even to someone else?"

LINDSEY: "Yeah, sometimes."

DR. G: "Okay, like about what? What would steam you?"

LINDSEY: "Well, I don't know. If I made a bad grade, I guess."

DR. G: "Okay, we'll get back to that one, but I mean more what other people do that steams you."

LINDSEY: "Oh. (long pause) Well, then, I guess when people lie to me. That makes me mad."

DR. G: "Okay, great. When have you felt people lie to you? How does that make you feel besides angry?"

LINDSEY: "I hate it. I really hate to be lied to . . ."

RITA: "Now, Lindsey. You know we mustn't say hate. That's an ugly word. You mustn't hate anyone."

LINDSEY: "But, Mom, that's how I feel when you and Daddy lie to me."

TOM: "Lindsey! Don't speak to your mother like that. We've never lied to you in your life. You shouldn't say that."

RITA: "No, sweetheart. How could you say such a thing about us in front of Dr. Gibbons? What will he think of us?"

LINDSEY: (*eyes down, softly*) "I'm sorry, Mom."

DR. G: "Don't be sorry, Lindsey. I want you to tell me exactly how you feel and what makes you feel that way. No matter what. I'm not here to judge any one, Rita. We're all here to find out about Lindsey's problem. Go on, Lindsey, when do you feel angry?"

LINDSEY: (*almost inaudibly*) "When they lie about loving me. They put on this act like we're one big happy family. Like we can talk and stuff."

RITA: "Lindsey! You know you can talk to me anytime."

LINDSEY: "I'm sorry, Mom, but that's not true. Daddy's hardly ever home, and you're always in the study working on some case. And even if you did have time for me, you don't care what I have to say. When I feel upset, you tell me I can't. It's not appropriate. When I'm mad, you say 'No, don't feel like that.' Just now when I said I hated to be lied to, you tell me I can't say hate because it's not nice. Well, Mom, maybe I can't say it, but I can sure feel it."

RITA and TOM: "Lindsey!"

RITA: "I'm terribly sorry, Dr. Gibbons. Lindsey usually is such a good girl. I don't know what's gotten into her. She's never acted like this before."

DR. G: "No, Rita. Instead of being allowed to have valid emotions and to express them, she's been instructed to repress them. She's chosen instead to control the situation through her refusal to eat."

TOM: "I'm sorry, Dr. Gibbons, but I'm having a little trouble swallowing this. You're saying that Lindsey's anorexia is caused by living in a happy family where people get along and don't argue? That seems strange to me. For my money, I think her mother's phobia about having a chunky daughter just went a little too far. That's all."

RITA: "I'm sorry, dear. Did you say my phobia? You're mistaken, I think. I wasn't the one who was so upset about Lindsey's weight. She was. Right, sweetheart? I have never let a word of criticism of our daughter pass my lips."

And therein lies a great part of the problem. Lindsey's family is too controlled and too controlling. She's grown up having to strap steel bands around her feelings. Never show anger, never say hate, never squeal with joy. And so in time, she learned how she could make herself feel nothing but the exhilaration of not succumbing to hunger and the power she alone had over her weight.

DR. G: "How do you feel about Lindsey's anorexia, Rita?"

RITA: "How do I feel? Why, I'm her mother."

DR. G: "But how do you feel about it? Does it concern you?"

RITA: "What an odd question. Of course I'm concerned about my baby."

Of course she's concerned, Dr. Gibbons is well aware of that, but how can Lindsey feel that concern? What troubles the therapist most, however, is the totally controlled tone, devoid of human feeling, that Rita has used to express this concern. She gives him "psychologically correct" responses spoken from the lips, not the heart. Lindsey's a smart young woman. She's been able to tell the difference between words and emotions for a long while.

Dr. Gibbons's job at this point is to reorder the family. One area they must work on is their interaction with one another. They must learn to feel and to express those feelings, to find joy in each other's triumphs and to commiserate with each other's failures. They've got a lot of unlearning and reeducation ahead of them in the healing of their outwardly perfect family unit. Establishing healthy family dynamics will expedite Lindsey's recovery. Even in the case of older patients, working through the disorder in a family therapy setting adds an important dimension. It does little good to work hard to recover on an individual level only to return to a disordered, unhealthy family setting. We'll delve a bit more deeply into the importance of creating a home environment conducive to healing in the next chapter. Let's move on, now, to examine the next aspect of the comprehensive treatment program: the medical evaluation.

The Medical Evaluation

Health History

Medical History—should include a complete review inquiring about her complaints in all body systems. A complete physical exam should be done to search for physical evidence of the disorder:

Eyes—Has she complained of vision disturbances? Seeing double? Is light painful? (These symptoms may be tip-offs to underlying blood-chemistry imbalances, such as low potassium, blood sugar, or excessive blood ketone levels.) Previous history of ruptured blood vessels around the eyes or in the whites of the eyes? (This symptom would usually occur from heaving and wretching with self-induced vomiting.)

Ears, nose, throat—Has she suffered frequent sore throats? Loss of hearing? Eardrum rupture? Hoarseness? Complained of loss of smell or taste? Suffered frequent bloody noses? (All these complaints could arise through prolonged or forceful vomiting episodes or from the caustic effect of even small amounts of acidic vomitus on the vocal cords and upper trachea.)

Lower respiratory (chest)—Previous history of pneumonias? Asthma? A persistent cough? (Again, it's possible to choke on the vomit and aspirate it—or suck it down—into the lungs. This can cause pneumonia, or could cause chronic irritation and inflammation that prompts coughing.)

Heart—Has she fainted? Complained of pain in the front of the chest? Or racing of the heart or skipping of beats? Any prior significant medical history involving the heart? For example, rheumatic (scarlet) fever in childhood can cause damage to the heart (leaving a murmur) or the kidneys. It's important to uncover as full a history for previous heart problems as is possible, because of the increased potential for underlying heart damage to cause rhythm disturbances that could be especially dangerous in a starved/malnourished state. Depending on her state of mental alertness, age, and level of cooperation, you may need to provide this information to a physician (be that a psychiatrist, general practitioner, internist, pediatrician), especially if that doctor has not cared for her in the past. (Fainting and rhythm disturbance of the heart may point to imbalances in blood chemistries or, in the case of purging through the use of syrup of Ipecac or other emetics, could portend heart muscle damage (cardiomyopathy) brought about by the toxic effect of chronic use of these substances.)

Gastrointestinal tract (stomach and abdomen)—Does she give a history of seeing blood in the vomit or bowel movements? Of vomiting material that looks like old coffee grounds (coagulated blood that has been acted on by stomach acid, often resulting from stomach ulcers)? Of bouts of diarrhea and/or constipation? Ever any episodes of bowel incontinence? (These symptoms, once again, usually result from abuse of laxatives or enemas, or as a consequence of self-induced, violent vomiting.)

Urinary tract—Is there a history of frequent infections of the bladder or kidney? Blood in the urine? Kidney stones? (The urinary tract is not an important target for problems brought on by eating disorders. However, chronic malnutrition can impair healthy immune function, and in women, the urinary tract is an easy mark for infection to take root. I do not intend to imply here that all women who suffer from frequent urinary tract infections should be considered highly suspect of disordered eating; there are a whole host of other causes. But, since malnutrition can occur in all three categories of disordered eating behavior, the incidence of its sequelae—in this case urinary tract infection—would reasonably also increase.)

Bones and joints—Does she complain of bone pain or aching joints? Has she suffered fractured bones, especially with minimal trauma? Do her joints swell? Do her feet and hands swell? (These signs could indicate loss of calcium and inadequate dietary replacement of essential amino acids and fats. Protein malnutrition can also contribute to retention of fluid in the feet and hands and abdomen.)

Muscles—Does she complain of cramping of the muscles? Weakness of muscle groups? Muscle twitches? These symptoms may be signs of insufficient amounts of potassium, calcium, or magnesium in the blood. These deficiency states could develop with chronic use of diuretic medications (water pills that anorectics and bulimics often take to lower their weight by fluid loss) or from excessive fluid loss through vomiting, enemas, or sweating with compulsive exercise.

Nervous system—Does she complain of numbness of the fingers, toes, hands, or feet? Any burning sensation of the soles of the feet or palms of the hands? (These sensations can be the result of certain vitamin and mineral deficiencies, especially among the B-vitamin group. With starvation, especially, deficiencies of vitamins in the B family and vitamin C occur because these are water soluble and, therefore, not stored by the body like vitamins A, D, E, and K are. Depletion of the required amounts of B-vitamin can lead to nerve "misfirings," often felt as burning pains in the feet and hands.)

Skin, nails, and hair—Has she noticed dryness of the skin or brittleness of nails or hair? Has she complained of new growth of fine hair over the body and face? Has she been easy to bruise? Bled longer than usual following a cut? Have wounds healed slowly or poorly? (In a state of malnutrition brought on by not eating, eating and purging, or eating the wrong foods, the levels of hormones—such as thyroid and reproductive hormones—necessary for the maintenance of these tissues falls. And after a sufficient amount of time, even the stored vitamins will finally become depleted. Vitamins A and E are important to hair, skin, and nails, and vitamin K to the normal clotting of blood.)

Family History

The family history should probe for occurrence of other relatives with addictive disorders, obesity, and depression or bipolar mood disorder (manic-depressive illness). The link between anorexia, bulimia, and compulsive overeating (or binge-eating disorder) and mood disorders, especially depression, is well established.[4] Particularly telling are first-degree relatives—i.e., a woman's mother, father, siblings, children—with major depression, panic disorder, agoraphobia, obsessive-compulsive disorder, and bipolar mood disorder. It may be that these disorders and the eating disorders share a common genetic, heritable link. The search for and proof of such a link has yet to occur, but the theory is sound.

Discovery of such a link may not be as far away as you might think. The federal government has pledged $62 million and another $3 billion over the next fifteen years in research funds devoted to unlocking these kinds of genetic secrets. The Human

Genome Project, as it has been named, has undertaken to identify in location and by function the entirety of the human genetic pool, which comprises many millions of genes controlling everything from the color of our hair to the potential to develop cancers—and possibly to a susceptibility for the development of eating disorders, too.

Gynecologic History

Because of the frequent occurrence of menstrual irregularities among disordered eaters, careful questioning about the timing, duration, and extent of menstrual cycles is important in their evaluation. In anorectics of long standing, virtually all will have ceased having periods completely. Bulimic purgers will usually exhibit some degree of irregularity, and frequently will also have suffered sufficient loss of hormonal function to develop amenorrhea (total absence of menstrual bleeding). The menstrual patterns for compulsive overeaters are all over the board: heavy periods of long duration, normal flow but irregular timing, some other permutation of flow and timing, or clockwork normalcy.

Gynecologic Evaluation

Except in teenagers who have never been sexually active, a comprehensive evaluation of any woman includes a pelvic examination and a Pap smear to detect cervical cancer, various viral infections of the cervix, ovarian cysts, or other growths.

If there is reason to suspect she has engaged in impulsive or promiscuous sexual behavior, or if there is a history of incest or other sexual abuse, routine testing for sexually transmitted diseases is a must. Such tests would include cervical swabbing to check for infection with chlamydia or gonorrhea, the swabbing and culture of any blisters or sores that are visible for bacterial infections or herpes simplex virus, and routine blood testing for HIV and syphilis.

Laboratory Evaluation

Blood chemistries

Multisystem blood chemistry profile—This bank of screening tests parades under a variety of names—among them SMAC, SMA-24, Chem Panel, Diagnostic Profile, and I'm sure a host of others. But all of them measure blood values to assess the function or status of the heart, kidneys, liver, pancreas, and bone; and check the levels of blood sugar, the electrolytes (like sodium and potassium), blood protein, blood fats (cholesterol and triglycerides), and usually uric acid and various minerals such as iron, calcium, and phosphorus. A thorough screening test like this one will quickly point up critically low potassium or blood sugar, early damage to muscles, heart, liver, kidneys, or bone, or developing protein malnutrition.

Complete blood count, or CBC—This test measures the size and number of the red blood cells to spot anemia from nutritional deficiency or other causes. It also measures the number and kind of white blood cells, which are the infection fighters. These immune-system blood cells could be reduced to dangerously low numbers in starvation or with some types of (especially viral) infections.

Thyroid studies—Normal functioning of this gland is critical in smooth metabolic control. Certainly, in some cases of obesity thyroid activity is low; however, in many it is not. In a starved state—which could occur, not only in anorexia, but in bulimic or compulsive overeating or binge-eating disorder—the metabolism downshifts to survive on the few calories coming in (on an ongoing basis in anorexia or during bouts of stringent dieting or fasting in bulimia or binge disorder) or on the few calories that stay long enough to do much good in vomiting bulimics. Only by this trick of metabolism (designed to help us survive in famine) could the "marvelous fasting maids" of history have been able to live for many months on tidbits of food.

The thyroid gland responds to metabolic or nutritional stresses through its output of the various types of thyroid hormone (T3, reverse T3, T4, T7, and free thyroxine). Its output depends upon stimulation from another pair of glands, the pituitary gland and the hypothalamus (remember our friend the hypothalamus, in which reside our feeding control centers?). When the body needs more thyroid hormone, the pituitary increases its output of TRH (thyrotropin-releasing hormone), which travels to the hypothalamus and tells it (chemical messengers again) to release its messenger called TSH (thyroid-stimulating hormone) which in turn travels to the thyroid gland itself and says "Supply more thyroid hormone, please!" We can measure the levels of these releasing hormones, too. In anorectics and bulimics, the TSH will usually be in the normal range, but its increased release in response to the call to duty from TRH is usually delayed or blunted. Interestingly, the same delay defect in this system occurs in patients with bipolar and depressive disorders. T3 will also usually be low in anorectics, and may occasionally be low in bulimics. However, this hormone always decreases under conditions of severe caloric restriction—which at times could apply to all the eating disorders—but returns to normal with a return to adequate nutrition.

Serum insulin—In cases of marked obesity that can result from compulsive overeating, the condition of insulin resistance can result. Chronically high levels of this hormone in the blood favor the vigorous laying down of fat, especially in the trunk and abdomen. This metabolic derangement probably does not have any connection with the development of the disorder, but may contribute in part to volatile blood sugars and the preferential craving for carbohydrate that triggers bingeing. If the level of insulin in the blood remains elevated after an eight- to twelve-hour fast, some degree of resistance is at work, and such patients need proper nutritional management to correct this insulin overload. Restriction of the intake of simple sugars and refined carbohydrates is important in correcting insulin overload in this kind of eating disorder.

Reproductive hormones—In anorexia of any significant duration, the levels of FSH (follicle-stimulating hormone) and LH (luteinizing hormone), which normally surge and wane to regulate the menstrual cycle, will be low. Thus, the invariable loss of normal menstrual cycling. The same situation develops in severe weight loss from any cause, and it is not known whether the reproductive hormone levels decline just because of the weight loss or because of some underlying biological derangement specific to anorexia. In bulimics, the level of LH is usually normal, but the FSH is sometimes decreased.[5]

Diagnostic Blood Tests

Dexamethasone Suppression Test—In this provocative test, the patient receives a dose of the synthetic corticosteroid dexamethasone; subsequently, her blood and urine are tested for the levels of cortisol they contain. Normally, this medication should suppress the release of the body's own cortisol into the blood and urine. In anorectics, bulimics, and in patients with depression or bipolar mood disorder, the test substance fails to suppress the release as it should. There has as yet not been sufficient study on this particular diagnostic test in binge-eating disorder to know whether this group also demonstrates failed suppression of cortisol release after the dexamethasone challenge. However, with the very strong correlation between this disorder and depression, it seems highly likely that such will prove to be the case. If so, this test could possibly be used, as it is in depressive illnesses, to target the risk for eating disorders among siblings, children, or other close blood relatives of a disordered eater. If such were the case, the benefit of such testing would clearly be in pinpointing those young women at risk and perhaps being able to prevent them from succumbing to an inherited biologic susceptibility for this syndrome.

Serum norepinephrine and serotonin (5HT)—Although these chemical neurotransmitters have proven quite useful in the research laboratory, so far they do not have a broad application in clinical practice. With the vast amount of research that is currently going on in this area, however, the documented differences that researchers have noted in the disordered-eating population may become useful as diagnostic tools in general use.

Toxicology

Because of their impulsive nature, bulimics may also abuse other substances, such as alcohol, marijuana, cocaine, diet pills, and emetic drugs such as syrup of Ipecac. A complete physical should include examination of urine and/or blood for the presence of toxic substances.

Cardiac Evaluation

EKG—The electrocardiogram, or tracing of the heart's electrical pattern, must be performed on every disordered eater, but is especially important for bulimics and anorectics. Because of the effects of Ipecac abuse and starvation, disordered eaters, especially in these two categories, can damage the muscle of the heart, making it weaker. There are also a certain subgroup of women (men, too) in whom the electrical system of the heart conducts slightly differently. In people who have this conduction abnormality—called a prolonged QT interval—the metabolic state of protein malnutrition can cause the development of fatal heart rhythms. When these arrhythmias occur, even the miracles of modern emergency cardiac technology cannot stop them. The abnormality is easily spotted on a standard EKG.

   Holter monitor—Physicians use this test, which amounts to a continuous EKG tracing over a twelve-, twenty-four-, or even forty-eight-hour period, to evaluate abnormal heart rhythms that show up on the standard EKG or to assess symptoms such as heart fluttering or fainting or sinking spells that patients may describe. It need not be used in all disordered eaters, but certainly, some physicians would recommend it if their history or physical evaluation seemed to warrant it.

Gastrointestinal Evaluation

Because of the abuse heaped upon the gastrointestinal system, especially by bulimics who purge through either vomiting, laxatives, or enemas, but also by bingers who overload the system beyond normal capacity, a thorough evaluation is in order. Evaluation should center on the lower intestine in those women who abuse laxatives or enemas. To perform this evaluation, the physician uses an endoscope, which is a lighted flexible tube, to look at the rectum and lowest part of the large intestine (a test called the proctosigmoidoscopy) or of the entire length of the colon (a full colonoscopy.) Conversely, these organs can be evaluated with a barium enema. Examination should focus on the esophagus, stomach, pancreas, and upper portion of the small intestine in bulimic vomiters (usually by an endoscopic examination, called the EGD, designed to look directly at the esophagus (*esophagó-*), stomach (*gastró-*), and upper intestine or duodenum (*duodenó-*) with a lighted flexible tube. Other tests that could be used to evaluate these organs are the barium swallow and upper GI X-ray examinations. In some cases, a full evaluation might also include a CT (Computerized Tomography Scan) or MRI (Magnetic Resonance Imaging Scan) scan of the abdomen, which are two kinds of X-ray scans that give detailed pictures of the internal organs enhanced by computer. The evaluation should include chemically testing the stool for blood in all disordered eaters, and if blood is found, further tests, such as those I just described, would be in order.

Dental Evaluation

Women who have purged through vomiting can severely damage the enamel of their teeth, leaving them vulnerable to attack by mouth bacteria and often riddled with cavities. Although the enamel loss sets the stage for this to occur, damage can also result from frequent bingcing on high-sugar foods, putting all bulimics as well as nonpurging binge eaters at risk for tooth damage. Untreated caries can lead to periodontal disease (inflammation and infection of the gums and tooth support structures), which can lead to loosening and loss of even sound teeth. Although stabilizing and treating more serious medical problems and getting control of the disordered eating patterns must take priority, repair of dental damage should also be a part of the complete treatment program.

Nutritional Evaluation and Reeducation

It would be untrue to say that most binge eaters, bulimics, and anorectics don't *know* what they're supposed to eat. For the most part, most of them are keenly aware of what they should be eating. Knowing and doing are not the same, however. There may be some of them, especially young teenagers, who have never really learned enough about what nutrients the body requires to make intelligent decisions and food choices. And in all of us, there's room for education. And so, part of a recovery program should provide solid information to educate—or reeducate—these young women in the basics of eating for good health.

In binge eaters and bulimics, the first order of business has to be to reestablish a sound, balanced nutritional rehabilitation plan. Because sugar and refined carbohydrates figure so prominently in bingeing, a plan that curtails the intake of these foods is important. Adequate intake of protein—on the order of 45 to 55 grams per day as a minimum for most women—will usually be enough to repair any damage that cyclic starving, purging, or excessive exercise might have caused. If an eating plan contains primarily lean protein sources, sufficient essential fats, a variety of nonstarchy vegetables, a limited amount of complex starches, and plenty of liquids, the metabolic signals for satiety will help to curb the urge to binge.

In anorectic patients, although the goal is going to be a steady intake of nutritionally sound foods, at first just achieving adequate intake of calories of any kind will help. Most anorectic women already restrict fat and sugar intake, albeit carried to the extreme, but may be deficient in other areas as well. Designing an eating program that will provide sufficient complete protein (one-half gram per pound of body weight would be ideal) in the leanest possible form will go a long way toward restoring the anorectic to a functional state both mentally and physically.*

---

* This program should also contain adequate fruits and vegetables to at least approach the Recommended Daily Allowance in vitamins and trace minerals.

Because the anorectic's satiety signals work over time already, adding in small amounts of foods that are higher in complex carbohydrate will in some cases help increase appetite a bit if she will accept them. The chief obstacle she will erect to making these modifications is her overriding fear of gaining weight. And so, nutritional rehabilitation in the anorectic must go hand in hand with work on the psychological and emotional components of her disorder.

Some medications can help to normalize the aberrant chemical messages in the brain that may cause or contribute to these disorders. Certain drugs seem to help stimulate appetite in anorectics, and now some newer medications have been released and others are currently under investigation that may help reduce binge urges in bulimics and binge eaters. Let's turn now to look at some of these drugs used in the treatment of eating disorders.

Drug Therapy

The drugs used to combat the symptoms of disordered eating fall into several broad groups. Some act to stimulate depressed appetite, some help to alleviate underlying depression and some act to curb the urge to binge. Let's look at each group for a moment.

Appetite stimulants—The prototype drug in this group is cycloheptadine (trade name Periactin), which acts in a fashion opposite to that of serotonin (5HT). Recall that serotonin acts in the feeding centers of the brain to induce a sense of satiety or satisfaction. Using a drug, such as Periactin, that in a sense counteracts the serotonin message should create a need to eat. And indeed that is precisely the basis for its use in the treatment of anorexia: to stimulate appetite. Although some early trial with the drug showed no greater improvement in food intake than that achieved with a placebo, a newer study seems to indicate that the original doses used were insufficient for the task. A study using larger doses (32 milligrams) shows at least some modest increase in food intake in anorectic women.[6]

Antidepressants—Studies have shown that drugs of the tricyclic antidepressant group appear to improve symptoms in bulimia and binge-eating disorder, and to some extent even anorectics. Although some trials with amytriptyline (trade name Elavil) and chlorimipramine (trade name Anafranil) showed little advantage over placebo in benefiting anorectics, these drugs do seem to help curb binge behavior in bulimics and compulsive overeating bingers. Studies have shown promising results in binge disorders and bulimia nervosa from not only medications in the tricyclic antidepressant class—(such as imipramine (trade name Tofranil) and desipramine (trade name Norpramin)—but from other antidepressant classes as well, such as trazadone (Desyrel) lithium carbonate, and the monoamine oxidase inhibitors (Nardil, Marplan, Isocarboxazide, Parnate). Of fourteen controlled trials using various antidepressants, twelve have shown significant positive results in the treatment of bulimia nervosa.[7]

The newer class of antidepressants, called serotonin reuptake inhibitors, seem to offer great advantages for sufferers of the bulimic and binge-eating disorders—as you might well imagine, with serotonin (5HT) tied so intimately into the feeding/satiety-regulating system. The drugs of this class, fluoxetine (Prozac) and its newer cousin, sertraline (Zoloft), act to increase the level of serotonin in the brain by preventing its reuptake. This action creates a net increase in the amount of seratonin for use. As you may remember from our earlier discussion, studies showed that bingers and bulimics exhibit a blunted or delayed release of serotonin after a carbohydrate-rich meal—i.e., these women don't release enough serotonin soon enough to switch the feeding signals to the "off" position on schedule. Making relatively more serotonin available should enhance the transmission of the "stop eating" signal. Indeed, it does appear that binge episodes become less frequent and that the associated depression seems to lift with the use of these drugs. Because of the recent furor over the drug Prozac, many readers may be reluctant to see their loved one use this medication. I encourage you to discuss these concerns with your own physician, as well as with the professionals helping your loved one recover, to try to come to a clearer understanding about the benefits versus the risk of this class of antidepressants. Drug choice in any condition must be individualized patient-to-patient and based on the clinical information and the situation at hand. The professionals charged with prescribing medications for an eating-disordered person are the ones in the best position to know if this or any drug would be worth the risk. From a clinical standpoint, however, I can categorically state that in my own experience in prescribing this drug, I have seen no examples of the kind of horror stories promulgated on television programs and in the news. That is not to say that Prozac could not sometimes cause bizarre and unpleasant side effects. The important point is this: become informed and weigh the help a drug could give in an illness against the potential for harm in that specific instance. It appears that in bingeing behavior, that benefit may be great.

Opiate antagonists—Drugs such as nalaxone (Narcan) had seemed in uncontrolled trials in the treatment of anorexia to offer some help, although in controlled studies they proved to be of only minimal benefit.[8] In theory, their potential for benefit in anorexia makes perfect sense because of the association between the natural opiates and feeding behavior that we explored earlier. Perhaps, as was the case with the antidepressant trials, the dose of opiate antagonist required to achieve good results in anorexia must be higher than what has thus far been used. Continuing research may indeed prove a benefit for drugs of this class, or as is so often the case, may open doors to the development of new drugs with greater efficacy or potency.

Antiseizure medications—Some research seemed to suggest that bulimia might represent a sort of seizure variant—i.e., the feeding behavior might be brought about by sudden abnormalities in brain wave activity in a manner analogous to the muscular jerking associated with the word *seizure*. ElectroENCEPHALOgrams, or EEGs (which trace the brain's electrical activity much like electro*cardio*grams trace the heart's electrical activity), have indeed demonstrated abnormal brain-wave patterns, at least in bulimia nervosa. Because of these findings, medical researchers have conducted trials using standard seizure medications to try to curb bulimic tendencies. In one small controlled study, phenytoin (Dilantin) seemed superior to placebo in reducing the frequency of binge episodes; however, after a time, two of the four women who did respond to the drug relapsed while still taking the drug. Uncontrolled studies with seizure drugs such as carbamazepine (Tegretol) and valproic acid (Depakene) have also shown some potential for benefit in bulimia; however, in most cases, the number of study subjects involved was small, and no data is yet available to support long-term benefit.[9] The association of aberrant brain waves and bulimia is an intriguing one, and I would expect further trials with these kinds of medications in the future.

On the Cutting Edge of Research

A few years ago, my husband and I attended the national scientific and research meeting of the North American Association for the Study of Obesity held in Bethesda, Maryland. At this meeting research scientists from all over the continent presented their current findings and work in progress involving the causes of obesity. Of the research work done on medications to reduce feeding behavior in the severely overweight—half or more of whom could more rightly be categorized as compulsive overeaters or binge-eating disordered—far and away the drug of the moment was one called d-fenfluramine (a relative of fenfluramine or Pondimin). The drug, which is not yet available to the general public, appeared in these studies to make significant inroads into overeating behavior in the morbidly obese. Small uncontrolled clinical trials have supported some benefit in controlling bulimia in nonobese women as well. This encouraging early work will, I hope, soon spur bigger controlled trials in the treatment of binge eating as well as obesity. Time will tell.

On the other side of that coin, the new drug Sumatriptan (Imitrex), which will soon be released for the control of intractable migraine headaches, may offer some hope to women with anorexia. This drug, which is a serotonin antagonist—i.e., blocks the action of serotonin—should function to counteract or at least to blunt the chemical message of serotonin in the brain that says to the anorectic: "You're full. Stop eating." Anorexia has so often proven refractory to treatment with medications, but perhaps this one will be the key.

What If Hospitalization Is Necessary?

Disordered-eating behavior occurs across a continuum of severity. Not every case responds to outpatient treatment. Some young women, especially those who suffer from anorexia or extreme bulimia, may at first require intensive therapy in a very controlled setting. In other cases, the family situation may not be one amenable to healing, or perhaps her relationship with someone in the home environment is contributing to the problem—i.e., in cases of parental drug addiction, alcoholism, or in cases of sexual or physical abuse. In such extreme situations, or of course when her disorder itself has placed her life or health in jeopardy, the professional counselor/therapist will most likely recommend hospital admission.

Ideally, she will recognize or can be persuaded to accept the need for intense help. But what if she does not? If the emergent nature of the disorder demands it, or if she is a minor, the decision may not be one you can leave to her. From a medicolegal standpoint, you simply cannot force her into therapy of any kind if she is a responsible adult. The key word in that sentence, however, is *responsible*. If she has become enmeshed so completely in her disorder that she is no longer thinking clearly, or if by her behavior she risks lethal complications, she is no longer acting rationally or responsibly. If you are her parent, sibling, or spouse, you may be forced to intervene in her behalf.

When it is possible, however, enlisting even her grudging acquiescence will improve her chances for recovery in treatment. Persuading her of this fact may not prove an easy task. Be prepared, especially in the case of anorectics, for some degree of resistance. The idea of ceasing her behavior means the risk of gaining weight, which is an unthinkable prospect to her. Recall the incident I referred to previously in which two anorectic women risked life and health by dumping their nutrient intravenous solutions into the sink and replacing them with tap water. It would be unusual for an anorectic, who absolutely does not view her behavior as abnormal or disordered, to freely admit a need for intervention at all, much less for hospitalization and feeding. You and the professional guiding you will need to be

both resourceful and persistent in the extreme to win her acceptance of the need for treatment in the hospital.

She may still refuse, and if she does, you must carefully weigh
the risks of her continuing the behavior against the trauma of
forcing the issue. If she is truly in danger—and your professional
counselor can help you determine if she is—there can be no
argument. However, in less extreme cases, the lines of necessity
may become blurred, and continual battling over the need for
inpatient treatment can prove more damaging than the illness in
some cases. Keep your long-range goal clearly before you at every
turn: that goal is to see her recovered and healthy, by whatever
method you and her therapist can manage.

If your efforts have succeeded in persuading her to enter an
inpatient treatment program, or if the emergent nature of her
disorder demanded admission with or without her approval,
what should you expect? During the weeks or even months that
you have striven to get her the help she must have, the focus of
your life has been on her and her disorder. Once she has been
admitted, you must relinquish responsibility for her care to the
program professionals. This separation is necessary to allow her
to adjust and is required in most inpatient facilities. She must
forge solid bonds of trust and confidence with the professional
staff in order to benefit maximally from therapy. Dependence on
family members or close friends can hamper this transference of
trust. And so, for a time, you will very likely be denied contact
with her. This phase of her treatment may be the hardest on you
and other concerned friends and family who have worked so
vigorously to get her into treatment. You may feel cut off and in
the dark, but I encourage you to respect the wishes of the professional staff and use the time apart from her to educate yourself
on how you can best help her when she is released.

Treatment Facilities Around the Country

An excellent reference book that I heartily recommend as a
sourcebook is titled *Controlling Eating Disorders*. The authors of

this publication have already compiled a comprehensive list detailing treatment facilities across the country, as well as outpatient programs, contact names, addresses, telephone numbers, and the kind of approach to the disorders offered by that program. This book will be an invaluable resource. In it, you will find a wealth of verified information already dug out, sifted, and waiting for you. If you cannot find this book through your local bookstore or library, or through a local chapter of one of the anorexia/bulimia self-help organizations, you may order a copy by calling the Oryx Publishing Company, 1-800-279-6799.

Chapter Seven

Healing the Home

Creating a Healthier Home Environment for Healing

Once you have succeeded in helping your loved one recognize that her behavior is a problem and accept the need for help, the work of healing has begun. If she is to spend some time in an inpatient program for recovery—or even if she is not—you should now take time to begin the process of healing the home she will return to or will continue to live in during recovery. Remember that you should view her disordered eating behavior as a symptom of stress in her life, and during the time she is beginning therapy, you and the other concerned family members and friends who have worked to help her so far must continue to help her by identifying the behaviors, stresses, and situations at home that may have contributed to her developing the behavior in the first place. It's also important for you to remember that you can't do anything about her behavior or her recovery—that's her job—but that you are in total control of your own behavior, work in therapy, and the way you choose to interact with her. I have already discussed the importance of both family and individual therapy in interpersonal healing, and the need to deal with alcoholism, drug use, physical or sexual abuse, and other contributing stressors, and I won't go into those areas again here. Suffice it to say that to ignore these family problems would be like calling a child in from play in a mud puddle, stripping off old soiled clothes, and putting on freshly washed, bleached, starched, and ironed ones without first giving the child a bath. The outside veneer would be clean and white and pretty, but the mud would still lie caked underneath, and soon it would soak through. If other family stresses exist, now is the time to confront them and to begin to heal these wounds. To ask her to do the work of recovery from her behavior alone without doing any work toward healing the family would be unfair and probably impossible if the goal is lasting change.

Identifying Problems in Letting Go

When you love someone, and you see them suffer—as you have watched your loved one suffer the torments of disordered eating—you want to help them and to keep on helping. For some people—particularly parents—this desire is especially strong. Parents often feel that they are to blame for the abnormal eating behavior in their children, and in some cases and to a certain extent, that feeling is justified. Their sense of guilt and need to "fix" the problem may stem from real fault, as with alcoholism, drug abuse, or parental knowledge of or commission of physical or sexual abuse. Or the feelings of guilt may derive from a situation in which the family has had a suffocating effect—a problem often seen in the family setting of anorectic women. Overwhelming closeness and lack of personal boundaries may have contributed to the problem in the first place, and it may prove to be a difficult behavior for others in the family to change. Whatever the cause, taking too much responsibility for your loved one's developing an eating disorder can lead to the problem of overinvolvement, and continued overinvolvement with her and her disorder can hamstring her recovery. Sometimes it's not so easy to know where to draw the line, to recognize when you've become too enmeshed with her disorder. Certainly, you can and should support her recovery efforts, but you absolutely cannot do it for her. How can you tell if you're becoming overinvolved? Let me give you a few examples that signal not being able to let go:

- secretly or overtly monitoring what she eats, counting her calories, making her food choices, constantly inquiring about her weight and her progress in recovery
- worrying so much about her disorder, her eating or her weight, that you ignore or neglect your home or work responsibilities, your marriage, your other children, or yourself.
- allowing her progress (or relapses) to determine how *you* feel.
- continuing enabling behaviors—i.e., not enforcing rules regarding food replacement, bathroom messes, or other house rules you've set as goals in recovery; reneging on the consequences of leverage if you used it in intervention; making excuses for continued engagement in disordered eating behavior

If you see yourself falling into these patterns, I urge you to stand apart from your own needs to control the "fixing" of the problem. Disengage your emotions, turn her recovery over to her and her counselor, and concentrate instead on the work of rebuilding a healthy relationship with her.

Rebuilding Relationships

During the stages of the eating disorder, the channels of communication among family members or friends may have shut down. In some cases, meaningful talk on topics other than food, weight, and eating may have ceased entirely. But as your loved one begins her journey down the road to recovery, you will want to begin the process of reestablishing the loving, close relationship you once had with her. To do this, you may have to learn to communicate with her on new terms.

Here are some ground rules for communicating that should help you get started:

1. Learn to *listen* to what she says. Be open to her views, gripes, needs, and opinions, whether you share them or not. Extend her

the courtesy of hearing what she says without passing judgment on it. Respect her right to her own ideas without criticism, just as you would hope she would respect yours.

2. Get to know her again. Discover (or rediscover) her likes and dislikes. Try to find some common ground with her, something you can both enjoy that is not connected in any way with food, weight, or eating. This could be an interest she has in art, movies, books, poetry, music, collecting, travel, pets, sports. It really doesn't matter what it is, as long as it is something that she enjoys or appreciates and that you can sincerely develop some interest in. By finding just a bit of common ground, one small thread of something you can share, talk about, and enjoy together, you can begin to reweave the tattered fragments of the fabric of your relationship with her.

3. Do not accuse, blame, or lay guilt about her behavior on her or anyone else. No matter what the provocation—even if she should backslide—never make statements such as: "Can't you see that you're hurting me?" or "What kind of person would act like you do?" or "If your mother finds out you're at it again, it will kill her" or "This whole thing is your fault." Try instead to speak in the first person: "I can see how hard you're trying." or "I heard you vomiting again last night, and it worried me. I'm concerned about you, and I'd like to help. Would you like to talk about what's bothering you?"

4. Allow open expression of feelings. In too many families—especially, but not exclusively, those of young women with anorexia—family rules forbid or curtail the expression of negative thoughts and feelings. It's the old _if you can't say something nice_ gambit—and remember that the anorexic profile is of a "good girl," a "nice girl" who aims to always please. But life and relationships are not always nice. Sometimes we all feel anger, resentment, or frustration that we need to express. Repressing or denying these natural feelings may prevent surface conflict within the family, but it won't stop the inner turmoil. Encourage and foster an environment in your home and family that allows

the rational expression of these negative emotions. Family members needn't resort to fisticuffs to express these feelings. It's perfectly OK to say: "I'm really feeling angry that you ate the entire cheesecake that was meant for tomorrow's dinner party. I don't like feeling this way" or "I am so frustrated at the mess you've left the living room in. I don't think it's fair of you to impose that way on the rest of the family" or "I wish you wouldn't borrow my favorite sweatshirt without asking me. That really ticks me off!" Only by being honest about how you feel can you hope to negotiate a compromise that will prevent continued bad feelings.

By the same token, express good feelings when they're sincerely felt: "I'm so happy that you made the finals in the class play" or "I'm excited about our trip to the zoo this weekend." The point is simply to begin to *feel* together again and to open the door to express all feelings—the positive or the negative—honestly.

Respecting Her Rights

The right to her opinion: Don't presume to know what she feels or what she needs. Talk about it. Even if she's a young teenager, she's capable of knowing her own mind and expressing her opinion. Don't attempt to choose or to think for her. Don't assume she doesn't want to have dinner. Don't assume she can't handle talking about her therapy or that she *needs* to talk about her progress. Don't assume she won't want to go to a birthday party where cake and ice cream will be served. All you have to do is ask: "We're having swordfish tonight. Would you like some?" or "I see Julie is having a birthday party. Would you like to go?" or "I'm interested in your progress with Dr. Smith if you would like to tell me." Respect her enough to allow her to make her own choices about what she does or does not want to do, how she does or does not feel, whether she does or does not want to share these feelings and thoughts with you or with anyone. Strive to make it clear to her that you're available to talk with her openly and with understanding acceptance when she's ready and if she so desires.

The right to privacy: Especially in families who have been enmeshed in the extreme, understanding and accepting the right to individual privacy may be difficult. However, it is crucial that within a family or group, no matter how close-knit, each person have a little time and space to call his own. It's possible to express concern and caring toward her or any person without seeming to intrude upon her personal boundaries. You may rightly feel that she has spent too much time apart from the family or her friends in the past, and for that reason you may be reluctant to ever see her go into her room and shut the door. Try to keep the issue of her need for privacy in perspective. As you slowly begin to rekindle the loving closeness you seek with her, remember to allow her the privacy she will need to digest and absorb the changes taking place in her own life and in her relationship to you and others.

On the other side of that coin, particularly if you are the parents of a disordered eater, you and your spouse, as a couple, need to draw some boundary lines of privacy within the family. You must take time out to devote solely to each other and to your relationship—time that has nothing whatever to do with her eating or her recovery. Rehabilitation of the strain that dealing with her disorder day in and day out may have wrought on your marital relationship demands some private time too. In other words, the respecting of rights in the family has to go both ways: you must respect her rights, and she yours.

The right to predictability and consistency: She has a right—and it's a crucial one—to know what to expect. All of us, children, teenagers, and adults, need to know whether a behavior will result in predictable consequences: If we do thing A, then we need to know that outcome B will result every single time. Lack of such predictability fosters a sense of confusion, helplessness, and insecurity.

My father—whose wisdom and beautiful, logical mind I miss every day—once told me what he thought was the key to raising happy, well-adjusted children. He said, "You don't have to make many rules, but when you do make one, you've got to make it stick." Some families tend to be chaotic, without established routines or consistently enforced rules at home. From the portrait of characteristics we painted in Chapter 1, you will recall that these traits occur most often in the families of bulimics; however, this group has no corner on the chaos market. If such is the case in the family of a disordered eater, however, the stress brought on by uncertainty about the world around her may contribute to her developing her own means of controlling the uncontrollable through food. If you see this kind of inconsistency in your dealings with her, you must begin to change that situation. Developing mutual trust takes time and effort, but the reward in building and healing your relationship will make the investment worthwhile.

Food Issues

Although, on the one hand, food is the central problem for the disordered eater, on the other, food is essential to the continuation of life, so neither you nor she can escape dealing with issues concerning food every day. Unlike the alcoholic or the drug addict, who can strive for total abstinence from the substances they have abused in the past, the anorectic, bulimic, or binge eater cannot ever achieve total abstinence from food. What they can—indeed, must—strive for, instead, is abstinence from practicing their abnormal behavior concerning it. Since this touchy subject must, of necessity, come up, how can you best handle it? Let me offer some basic ground rules.

1. Avoid confrontations over food. Try not to focus on what your loved one eats or refuses to eat. Absolutely do not make comments encouraging her to eat more, eat less, eat something different. Let her work through these issues in therapy. What you desire at mealtime is her company, her participation in family conversation and communion. So when a meal is ready to eat, ask her to join you. Ask what, if anything, of it she would like to eat, but accept what she says without judgment.

For example, in the case of Lindsey, the young anorectic you met previously, her mother might say, "Lindsey, it's time for dinner. Will you join us?" If Lindsey says she would rather not eat, then her mother should respond with something along the lines of, "That's fine. You don't have to eat, we'd just like your company at the table." If she still refuses, her mother should let her know the invitation remains open for another evening and drop it. She should neither beg nor plead for her presence, nor remind her that she's supposed to be trying to eat more in her recovery program. Neither should her father join in with remarks such as: "Can't you see what this is doing to your mother? The least you can do is sit down and *try* to eat something!" Any of these responses would negate all good feeling that may have begun to develop, and return food and her anorexia to the forefront of family life.

But what if Lindsey did choose to join her parents at the table? Her mother should simply offer the meal without even the appearance of forcing any part of it to her plate. Neither parent should make comments about the size of portions she takes, the fact that she chooses only a little spoon of green beans and some salad but eschews the chicken breast, the peas, the milk, and the dessert. Letting go of the need to help her by making food decisions for her is difficult—especially for a parent—but is critically necessary. Let her do it and focus your energies and attention on building and maintaining a healthy, open, and loving relationship with her.

2. Reevaluate the purchase and preparation of food. Many anorectics not only enjoy talking about food, they enjoy preparing full meals for other people to eat. If she enjoys doing so, and if her therapist agrees that it would not be counterproductive to her recovery, allow her to continue to do these things. In the case of adult bulimics and bingers, however, having to shop for groceries and prepare meals for the rest of the family may prove stressful enough to trigger binge episodes. If this is the case, someone else in the household should take over these food-related duties for her.

Whoever does take on the grocery shopping and cooking duties should not feel that the rest of the family must avoid typical foods she has binged on in the past—cookies, cake, donuts, ice cream, sweets—to "save" the disordered eater from temptation. It would not save her any more than refusing to keep alcohol in the home would prevent an alcoholic from seeking out a source elsewhere. The family's grocery-buying habits should continue as usual. Although for the sake of good health, all of us would be better served to forgo the regular consumption of a diet of high-sugar foods, forcing the entire family to give up treats in their own home would be unfair and would serve only to make the other household members resent her and her disorder all the more. Do not suppose that she would not feel the weight of their resentment upon her. She would.

A good compromise, especially for households of bulimics and binge eaters, is to allow each family member a small allotment of the monthly food budget to select special food items that he or she would enjoy. This process should include the disordered eater as well, without editorial comment or judgment on the choices she makes. These special items and a share of the communal food become the property of each person sharing the house, and they each place their share of food on a marked shelf. Use of food from another household member's shelf without permission is deemed off limits. And even with permission, each person must replace any food eaten from someone else's shelf. Adhering to this kind of plan would in theory eliminate battles over missing food and would prevent resentment from taking root over denying others in the house access to food they would enjoy to eat. However, the method will work only if the family enforces rules regarding the sanctity of other people's property (food) and the mandatory replacement of borrowed food.

3. Food preparation should also continue as it always has. Continue to serve the same kinds of foods that the remainder of the household enjoys with as little overt alteration as you can manage. In the case of anorectics, it is futile to try to tempt her with delicacies that you think she might like. Instead, try asking and observing. What does she *say* she would eat? What do you see her eat? Although you don't want to appear to alter the family's normal menu to suit her disordered habits, you may find she is more accepting of meals lower in fat, of lean meats that are broiled or baked and not fried, and of fresh salads, fruits, and vegetables. These are changes that you can most likely accomplish without a major overhaul of food choices.

Certainly, on the surface, these food choices make pretty good dietary sense. But I would caution you not to go overboard in making such changes in food preparation. The well-meaning families of many obese compulsive overeaters or bulimics make the mistake of serving fare when she joins the table that suggests a weekend at a low-fat diet camp: a sliver of overcooked skinless chicken breast, a handful of cooked carrots, a small spoon of beets, and a glob of cottage cheese with a parsley garnish. Yuk! She may sit down and pick at that offering, but all the while, she probably dreams about the half-gallon of fudge ripple ice cream she's going to get at the store when she's excused from the table. And she will definitely recognize that it's not the same juicy stuffed baking hen with whipped potatoes, gravy, cranberry relish, three-bean salad, rolls and butter that normally would have been there.

Aim for minor modifications—keep the baking hen, add well-seasoned green beans or grilled squash in place of the whipped potatoes, or even keep the whipped potatoes, perhaps in smaller quantity. In short, try to prepare and serve food the entire family can enjoy, ask for her company, and let her choose what she will have of the meal. If she would like something else, then fine. Allow her to prepare something of her own choosing, but absolutely do not do it for her. She must begin to be responsible for her own choices and for reordering her food attitudes. If you alter your patterns to make these choices for her, she's accomplished nothing, and the message you've sent is that you find her incapable of making even the simplest decision herself.

Setting Realistic Nutritional Goals at Home

For Anorectics

The primary goal of increasing calories is especially important if she has practiced stringent restriction sufficiently long to reach a dangerous weight. However, once refeeding has allayed immediate concerns about her safety, attention can turn toward rebuilding her health. I will outline for you (and for her) the minimum amounts of the basic nutritional building blocks that her diet should provide. Remember, however, that although it may be helpful for you to have some factual information about her nutrition, and certainly it's important that she know and understand these nutritional guidelines, let me underscore one warning: *You cannot do this for her!* You must not pressure her to eat more of her meat, that she has not had enough calcium, that she should try to eat some more cereal. She would balk at your attempt to control her diet and you would find yourself back at square one in recovery. If you are a parent or a spouse, then you can use the information to help in preparing family meals so that you'll be at least offering her adequate nutritional support. (Remember not to make drastic changes in the family's normal diet, however.) She has to be the one to determine her level of intake and to make informed choices about what she should eat. It is her health and her recovery.

Protein intake: Her first and most important need is for protein sources. These can be lean meat; poultry, fish, or eggs; or dairy products such as milk, cheese, or yogurt. Although you can find protein sources from the vegetable world, most of them, alone, are not complete proteins and are therefore not adequate to replace protein stores on an ongoing basis. All vegetable sources of protein lack one or more of the essential amino acids (the basic protein building blocks that the body cannot manufacture by rearrangement of other amino acids and must have regularly for good health), and these deficiencies require that you match two or more vegetable or grain protein sources to achieve completeness.

Although anorectics often report that they dislike the fatty taste of meats and prefer not to eat foods prepared with animal grease or oil, they may accept egg white or milk products, both of which provide excellent protein sources. In fact, the white of the egg is the gold standard against which all protein sources are measured for completeness. If your loved one, for whatever reason, eschews all animal protein sources including eggs and milk products, vegetable protein matching is your only alternative. In that case, let me recommend a book titled *Diet for a Small Planet* (Ballantine, 1982), in which you will find a wealth of information on how to eat a vegetarian diet that is still complete in all essential amino acids.

The daily intake of complete protein depends upon weight. Let me give you a rough but easy method of calculation: Each pound of body weight demands a protein intake of one-half gram daily. By that calculation, a 100-pound woman would need to eat 50 grams of complete protein per day for good health. The calculation actually derives from lean body weight, which is the weight of the body with all fat stripped away. However, in a practicing anorectic, who may have a very low body-fat percentage, the approximation comes close.

Carbohydrate intake: Although anorectics need to consume adequate protein, they must counterbalance the appetite-sating effect of protein and fat by beginning to increase their intake of complex carbohydrates as well. Although she will very likely choose to avoid heavy, sugary foods—she could begin with some of the lighter starches, such as oats or rice in the form of cereals or in bread, muffins, or crackers, and those found in the cruciferous vegetables (cabbage, cauliflower, broccoli and mustard greens) and legumes. And she can also add some of the simple carbohydrates found in fresh fruits.

Begin at a low level and aim for a total of 70 to 100 grams of carbohydrate (or a bit more if she will accept it) each day. A rapid increase in the carbohydrate load may make her balk, for two reasons: first she will gain weight (both from increased fat deposition and from fluid retention), which she will resist, and second, she will feel bloated or gassy and may develop stomach cramping. The fiber content in the oats and such vegetables as broccoli, green leaf salads, asparagus, cauliflower, and dried beans or peas causes this phenomenon, and it is especially pronounced at a time of rapid increase; thus the importance of *slowly* increasing the amounts of these fibrous foods. As she becomes accustomed to the level of fiber, the bloated and crampy feeling should pass.

Fat intake: Here is where you will meet the most stalwart nutritional-recovery resistance from your loved one if she is anorectic. However, just as is the case with protein, some fat (a fatty acid, more precisely) is absolutely essential for good health. This fat is called linoleic acid, and our bodies—especially her starved one—need a small amount of it daily to function as a precursor framework from which to build many of the hormones, anti-inflammatory prostaglandin compounds, and cell walls throughout the body. Even small servings of animal fat found in lean meats or poultry, fatty fish (such as salmon, mackerel, herring, sardines), egg yolk, or butter (milk) fat will provide sufficient amounts of essential fat for good health.

Again, if you meet granite resistance to animal fats of all types, vegetable oils (such as olive, canola, corn, safflower) will fill the bill. You may have to disguise fats and oil of any kind in cooking if she dislikes the oily or greasy quality. Or she could even take her essential fats in capsule form. A product called Omega Syn (made by Bio Syn, Inc., a company in Marblehead, Massachusetts), an encapsulated vitamin and fat supplement rich in essential fats and omega fatty acids and antioxidants, will help to provide the needed fat in what she may view as a more palatable form.

Vitamins—In addition, since she has deprived herself for an extended period, she will likely have become quite deficient in vitamins, trace minerals, and iron. Replacement of these vital nutrients is important. Unless her medical evaluation turned up some specific deficiency (iron-deficiency anemia, B^{12} and folate deficiencies, and the like), a single multivitamin and mineral-replacement tablet (available over the counter) that is complete in the Recommended Dietary Allowances (or RDA) for these substances is adequate. Specific deficiencies require more vigorous therapy to restore sufficient amounts, and that usually requires a prescription supplement from her physician.

For Bulimics

Devising a sound nutritional plan for a bulimic does not require many significant changes from the basic needs I just outlined for her anorectic cousins. The goal is to work nutritionally *with* her biology. Keep in mind the altered response to the sating effect of some foods, the imbalances and delays in release of certain brain chemicals that you learned about in earlier chapters.

Protein intake: As with anorectics, the bulimic's daily requirement for complete protein—sources providing all the essential
amino acids in adequate amounts—is one-half gram per pound
of lean body weight. In most cases, working from the total body
weight in practicing bulimic purgers will get you close—perhaps
erring on the high side, but for protein, better slightly too much
than too little. By this calculation, a rough "guesstimate" of 60
grams of protein a day would suffice for a 120-pound woman.
You could derive a more accurate number by figuring the lean
body weight and using that figure in your calculation of daily
protein need. (In the next section, on nutrition for compulsive
overeaters, I will note some resources that give you accurate and
simple methods to calculate lean body weight.) Nitrogen-balance
studies are laboratory measurements that determine protein
need based on how much her body uses versus how much she
consumed in a day, and would certainly give the most accurate
value of all, but these are impractical except in the hospital setting.

Because the levels of the brain chemical messenger serotonin,
or 5HT, fail in the bulimic (and binger) to rise as rapidly as
necessary in response to a dietary carbohydrate load to effec-
tively shut off the hunger signal, a bulimic may need to rely on a
different messenger system. Gut peptides (messengers much like
the neuropeptides in the brain but released by the gut instead)
also rise in response to protein and fat entering the stomach and
act to sate the appetite. In the absence of a strong enough message from the brain, cholecystokinin (or CCK, as it is more commonly called) may have to carry the day in transmitting the "stop
eating" signal. To that end, eating a diet rich in protein sources
and with a modestly higher fat content may stimulate the release
of CCK at the gut level and help to curb the desire to binge.

Carbohydrate intake—Certainly, foods from this category are the
ones she has most likely abused through bingeing. (This is probably also true for women who suffer from binge-eating disorder
but do not purge.) She may have tried—through carbo binges—
to whip some response out of her sluggish brain chemicals to
achieve the calming effect she seeks. Turning off her craving for
binge food will never be an easy task for her. But certainly, eating

a diet that limits her intake of refined sugars (table sugar, powdered sugar, honey, and foods or beverages in which these are the
primary ingredient) and starches (processed white flour and
foods in which it is the primary ingredient) will help. These kinds
of carbohydrates play havoc with blood sugar and with brain
chemicals; once eaten, refined sugars and starches will fuel her
desire to stuff herself with more of the same.

She should eat some carbohydrates of the complex variety—
whole-grain cereals, high-fiber vegetables such as broccoli, fresh
salad greens, cauliflower, asparagus, green beans, and legumes.
She should try to spread her intake of starches out so that she
doesn't consume large amounts of carbohydrate at one sitting.
These complex starches also have a sating effect on hunger
brought about by their bulk. Too much bulk in her stomach at
once may serve to remind her keenly of the stuffed "full and
happy" feeling she learned to associate with her bulimia—just
prior to going over the top and feeling the need to purge. I would
aim for a daily intake of complex carbohydrates in the neighbor-
hood of 60 or 75 grams. At that level, most women can maintain
their weight without much effort, and it is a level that should
provide sufficient nutritional support.

The most important aspect of any nutritional plan for a bulimic or for a binger is that she learn to listen to her body's needs.
To learn to recognize the difference between physiological hunger and *psychological* hunger, she must be patient, persistent, and
willing.

Vitamins and minerals—Especially because of her purging tactics, she may have developed deficiencies in potassium, in chlo-
ride, in iron, and in essential vitamins. Even once the binge/
purge episodes have waned or stopped, it will take some time to
restore the low levels of such vital nutrients to normal. In many
cases, her physician may recommend replacement of potassium,
magnesium, calcium, iron, vitamin C, and the B-vitamin group
through supplements. If no specific deficiency has yet occurred,
she should do fine on just a single complete multivitamin and
mineral that contains the RDA for these micronutrients.

Fiber—In the bulimic who has purged through laxatives or
enemas, reestablishing normal colon (large intestine) movement
may prove difficult. Eating a diet that provides sufficient fiber

will help prevent the constipation that a sluggish overmedicated or overworked bowel may develop. By eating foods rich in dietary fiber (oats and other whole grains, cruciferous vegetables, green leafy vegetables, orange and yellow vegetables, and some fresh fruits), she should be able to work up to a daily intake of fiber on the order of 35 to 40 grams per day. If her intake of foods to provide this amount of fiber falls short, she may supplement her intake with powdered bulk vegetable-fiber products, such as Metamucil or Konsyl, which contain no chemical stimulants for the intestines. The only drawback in the use of these products is that she may fall into the old habit of taking too much too often, especially if she has abused laxatives in the past. And so I make a qualified recommendation for their use.

She should make all changes in fiber intake slowly, because as I mentioned before, rapid increases in fiber consumption may spark bouts of bloating, intestinal cramping, and gassiness. Any of these may tap into old signals that call for a need to purge.

For Compulsive Overeaters

Nutritional recommendations for women who suffer from the binge-eating disorder vary according to their degree of weight gain. The health consequences of extreme overweight threaten the binger just as the consequences of starvation threaten the anorectic. Although the problems these two disorders create may differ, both cause valid medical concerns.

For the morbidly obese binger, developing a sound nutritional plan that works with her disordered metabolism (along with medications, counseling, and self-help support) to curb her binge behavior will offer her the best chance for restoring her emotional *and* physical health.

The information I have already presented for the bulimic with regard to carbohydrate, protein, and fat intake applies to these women who also binge but do not purge, although they do not generally have the added problems created by purge tactics— electrolyte imbalances and nutrient deficiencies. Let me elaborate on a few areas of difference.

Protein intake—In figuring her daily protein requirement, you should try to base your calculation upon her lean body weight and not her total weight. Since many morbidly obese overeaters may weigh 250 or 300 or more pounds, the rough approximation of one-half gram per pound would require her to eat 125 to 150 grams of protein per day. Her lean body weight, however, most likely falls somewhere near 120 or 130 pounds once you subtract the weight of fatty tissue. You can find step-by-step instructions on how to calculate lean body weight with nothing more than a scale, a measuring tape, and pencil and paper in the book *Thin So Fast* by Michael R. Eades, M.D. (Warner Books, 1989) and in *How to Lower Your Fat Thermostat* by Remington, Fisher and Parent (Vitality House International, Inc., 1983). Armed with this information, you can arrive at a realistic protein requirement for her daily intake.

Carbohydrate intake—One of the health consequences of bingeing on carbohydrates becomes especially important when dramatic gains in body fat occur. Not only do these women (and men) have abnormalities in the chemical messengers that control hunger, but their metabolic system operates a little differently, too. In the face of a high intake of carbohydrates—complex starches, refined starch and sugar, and simple sugars—they develop the problem of insulin resistance that I spoke about earlier. This defect in metabolic control, which occurs gradually over their lifetime (it usually does not trouble them in childhood and adolescence, or at least they are spared the consequences of it until later), creates a different nutritional need for carbohydrates. For these individuals, not only do the carbohydrate binges set up the vicious cycle of eating and then wanting more, as they do for bulimics, but since these women do not purge, each heavy load of incoming carbohydrate worsens their insulin resistance and its metabolic consequences—the laying down of central body fat, high blood pressure, fluid retention, atherosclerotic heart disease, and diabetes.

One of the challenges these women face in recovery is the rehabilitation of their disordered metabolism along with their disordered relationship with food. Standard low-calorie dieting usually only makes these women feel hungrier, deprived, and more depressed—but that should not surprise you when you consider the fact that standard low-calorie diets consist mainly of carbohydrates, which keep the insulin levels up, which further fuels the underlying metabolic problems, which keeps the cycle in motion. Reordering the abnormal eating patterns in the obese binge eater demands severe restriction of incoming carbohydrate to a level of sometimes as low as 10 grams per day until the physician monitoring her nutritional program can see signs that consequences of her disordered metabolism—the basic underlying defect of which is abnormal insulin metabolism—have come under control. Then the level of complex carbohydrate she will be able to tolerate can come up to the level of nonobese bulimics (i.e., about 40 to 60 grams per day, depending on how resistant she had become).

For most bingers, nutritional rehabilitation can occur on a full food-eating plan that allows her plenty of protein and even some fat to sate her hunger, and limited only in carbohydrate intake. On such an eating program, even on a substantial number of calories, metabolic reordering will allow her blood pressure, blood fats, blood sugar, and weight to return to normal levels.

For any disordered eater—anorectic, bulimic, or binger—the first and most important goal in recovery must be to disengage her from the distorted relationship she has developed with food from a psychological standpoint. This occurs in therapy with her counselor and through her ongoing hard work. Once this work has reduced and finally abolished the abnormal eating patterns, the business of nutritional rehabilitation using the guidelines I have given you above will help restore your loved one to better health.

Maintenance

Relapse Awareness

As with any addictive disorder, the possibility of her returning to the disordered behavior exists. It is real, and both she and you must be keenly aware of it. Recovering alcoholics fall off the wagon, reformed smokers resume smoking, ex-junkies return to drug use. It can happen to anyone who fails to maintain a constant awareness and vigilance for signs of falling back into their old patterns. That's why one of the principles of recovery from any substance or behavior is: *Always recovering, never recovered.* Protecting her hard-won recovery will demand a day-to-day, even a moment-to-moment commitment to abstinence—on her part and on yours. But wait a minute! What do I mean by *yours*? Haven't I said that her recovery to this point is her struggle alone? Shouldn't, therefore, her commitment to day-to-day maintenance be hers alone? What am I bringing you into this battle for?

You're absolutely right in that thinking. She and she alone can make the daily choices of maintaining abstinence from her previous abnormal eating behavior or of returning to it. And it is exactly this point that I ask that you remember every moment of every day. *She is responsible for her recovery and you are responsible for yours.* You are responsible to protect and cultivate the healthy relationship that you have begun to develop with her. You are responsible for your own happiness. You are *not* responsible for her abstinence from disordered eating. You should not act as her police officer, her overseer, or her judge. What you can do for her, however, is to work together to set into place a feedback system to help signal either of you if you begin to slip back into the abnormal relationships you once had.

Spotting: The Feedback System

Have you ever marveled at ballet dancers or ice skaters making rapid pirouettes? If you have, you may have wondered how they could spin around and around so fast without getting dizzy. As a child, you may have tried it and staggered and fallen for your effort. The dancer or the skater, however, has learned an important secret: feedback. These artists choose a spot of reference that doesn't change, and they fix their sights on it. As they begin the spin, they "spot" that fixed point and they don't take their gaze off it until the turn forces them to, and then they bring their gaze immediately back to the spot from the other direction. By "spotting" they can maintain their orientation and balance even while spinning like a whirling dervish. In her recovery and in yours, you should choose such a spot (or group of spots) for yourself. Your "spots" could be, for example, the professional counselor you've worked with, a respected friend or family member, a teacher or clergy member, or the members of a self-help support group you attend.

Although once firmly on the road to recovery, neither of you will require contact as frequently with the professional counselor who has guided her back, these ties should remain firm. Periodically, although less often, she (and you) should plan regular sessions with the therapist to touch base, to continue to work, and to get a reality check. The professional therapist is in an excellent position to be a "spot" for you, to give you unwavering feedback on how firm your footing on the recovery road really is. From a more detached perspective, he or she may pick up on small clues, nuances of behavior, slight changes in attitude too subtle for those of you intimately involved in the relationship to see clearly. These minute differences could signal that your balance has begun to become uncentered. Alertness for even a small degree of slipping back into old ways of thinking, reacting, and behaving can identify centering problems when they are small, more easily corrected, and less painful to confront and repair.

But your therapist is only one of the potential "spots" I mentioned. Anyone can serve you and your loved one in this capacity, but a good spot has to be able to give you their nonjudgmental opinion about questions you bring to them, and tell you hard truths without fear or hesitation. Think about the dancer. She would fall if she looked at this spot now and some other spot on her next revolution, always changing the spot for expediency's sake. And you and your recovering disordered eater, by the same token, would relapse into old habits, old coping tools, and your old disordered relationship if you chose "spots" that were not wholly truthful in dealing with you or if you failed on your end to accept their frank opinion. Your part of the bargain, your commitment to the system, is to be completely honest with your spots and to accept what they tell you as truth without anger or hurt feelings.

Don't get into the trap of searching out a group of "yes" spots who want to please you by telling you everything is dandy even when they can see your spin unraveling and know a fall is imminent. If dancers chose spots on revolving walls, ones that moved between looks, the stage floor would be littered with a tangle of dizzy dancers. Choose your feedback spotters with care and vow to listen to them even when they tell you things you've been trying to deny. Preservation of her recovery and of yours hangs in the balance.

What If She Does Relapse?

If your feedback spots tell you the spinning is out of whack, gone haywire again, what should you do? Throw your hands up and say "I tried. Oh, well. I guess it just didn't work" and give up? No. Absolutely not. If the dancer falls, he gets back up and finds the spot and begins to spin again.

Relapsing into old habits signals that the work is not yet complete on her part or yours. It means that she has not yet disengaged from her reliance on disordered behavior as a response to stress cues. When the going gets tough, she retreats into the familiar, even though the familiar is unhealthy and abnormal. A relapse signals underlying stresses that she's having trouble dealing with in an appropriate way. It runs up a red flag of warning about stressors in her life and her relationships. View a relapse as a cry for help. Don't give up on her.

You, like the fallen dancer, must pick yourself up and begin again. And she must do the same, although she may not see it immediately. This time, it may take only a discussion with her to help center her again, to get her back into regular therapy, and back onto the road to recovery. Or, it could require another intervention if the seriousness of the relapse warrants it, and she has not responded appropriately to your attempts to center her. If that is what is to be, with the help of your professional return to the steps I outlined for you and try again. The likelihood of success is just as great this time, perhaps even more so, because you know her better, you know the process better. She's still the loved one you sought to help the first time. She simply needs your help again. Don't give up on her recovery.

I do want to mention at this point that now and again a disordered eater has become so dependent and addicted to the behavior that try though you might, she will not respond. I have encouraged you throughout this book to keep trying, not to give up on her and the hope for her recovery, and I honestly mean for that to be your goal. But what about those cases when the family, friends, and spouse have given their best efforts to bring her to treatment again and again and have been unable to succeed? Does the time ever come when you must cry "Uncle"? I would hope not too quickly or easily for her sake and yours, but the answer is yes. If, with the help of counselors, clergy, friends, and family she remains stalwartly planted in her disorder, and when the attempts to free her begin to strain your resources and to rob the quality of your own life, it may be time to admit your limits have been reached. Your own sanity, relationships with others, financial security, and health are equally important. If this should happen to you in your hope to free your loved one from disordered eating, return to the Twelve Steps program I outlined for disordered eaters. Learn to offer up the care of her disorder into the hands of a Higher Power. Release yourself—and you may need a great deal of support from your counselor, your friends, your other family members to do this—from the sense of personal responsibility you have assumed on her behalf. You can still hope for her recovery, but you simply can't let her problem destroy you or others you love. In this instance you must let it go and go on with your life.

Postscript

Once she's finally free from disordered eating, that fragile freedom becomes a treasure to protect, to defend, and to preserve. Both you and she must maintain your center and your balance to keep on spinning. Give yourself a good daily dose of humility—the kind that comes from recognizing that this kind of problem can affect anyone, the small and the tall, the mighty and the meek. Share your recovery with others who struggle now in the tangled undergrowth of disordered eating, searching for the road head. Help them out onto that road that you and she have traveled together. Remember, you're still travelers, just farther along where the road is smoother.

Notes

Chapter 1

[1] Farley, Dixie, "Eating Disorders Require Medical Attention," *FDA Consumer,* Vol. 26, No. 1, March 1992, pp. 27–29.

[2] Kelly, John T., M.D., "Bulimia Nervosa," *Medical Tribune,* April 14, 1988, pp. 17–19.

[3] *Diagnostic and Statistical Manual of Mental Disorders,* ed. 3, revised, Copyright American Psychiataric Association, Washington, D.C., 1987.

[4] The BMI is a standardized measure of weight to height that allows researchers and physicians to compare diverse groups of people on a standard scale. For example, a woman of 140 pounds at 5'5" is quite different from one standing 5'10" at that weight.

[5] Table 1 is taken from Fig. 25.4-1, Nomogram for Body Mass Index, *Comprehensive Textbook of Psychiatry/V,* Vol. 2, Ed 5, p. 1179.

[6] Pope, Harrison, and Hudson, James, "Eating Disorders," *Comprehensive Textbook of Psychiatry/V,* Vol. 2, Ed 5, p. 1859.

[7] Because the syndrome has yet to settle definitively on a name, please indulge my interchangeable use of the terms *compulsive overeater, overeater, binge eater, and binger* to identify women who suffer from the binge-eating disorder.

[8] Brody, Jane, "Study Defines 'Binge Eating Disorder,' " *The New York Times,* March 27, 1992, p. A16.

[9] Lomax, James, M.D. "Obesity," *Comprehensive Textbook of Psychiatry/V,* Vol. 2, ed. 5, pp. 1180–1182.

Chapter 2

[1] Brumberg, Joan J., *Fasting Girls: The History of Anorexia Nervosa,* Penguin: New York, 1989.

[2] Pope, H., and Hudson, J., "Eating Disorders," *Comprehensive Textbook of Psychiatry/V,* Vol. 1, Ed. 5, pp. 1856–1857.

[3] Laurence, Leslie, "Eat What You Love—Without Feeling Bad," *McCall's,* May 1992, p. 80.

[4] Yates, A., "Current Perspectives on the Eating Disorders," *Journal of the American Academy of Child and Adolescent Psychiatry,* Vol. 28, 1989, pp. 813–828.

[5] Brewerton, T., et al., "Dysregulation of 5HT Function in Bulimia Nervosa," *Annals of the New York Academy of Science,* Vol. 575, 1989, p. 501.

[6] Yates, Allen, "Current Perspectives on the Eating Disorders," *Journal of the American Academy of Child and Adolescent Psychiatry,* 1989, pp. 813–825.

[7] Leving, Allen, and Billington, Charles, "Opioids: Are They Regulators of Feeding?" *Annals of the New York Academy of Sciences,* 1989, Vol. 575, pp. 209–215.

[8] Brumberg, Joan J., *Fasting Girls: The History of Anorexia Nervosa,* Penguin: New York, 1989.

[9] Blumenthal, J., "Is Running an Analogue of Anorexia Nervosa? An Empirical Study of Obligatory Running and Anorexia Nervosa," *JAMA,* Vol. 252, 1984, pp. 520–523.

[10] Seasonal affective disorder, or SAD, is an illness of mood in which periods of depression, carbohydrate craving, excessive sleeping, and weight gain occur in cycles when there is less sunlight. The symptoms appear in the fall and winter and vanish in the spring and summer.

[11] Wurtman, R. and J., "Carbohydrates and Depression," *Scientific American,* January 1989, pp. 68–75.

Chapter 3

[1] *Synopsis of Psychiatry: Behavioral Sciences, Clinical Psychiatry,* Kaplan, Harold, and Sadack, Benjamin, eds., Baltimore: Williams & Wilkins, 1991.

Chapter 6

[1] Pope, Harrison, and James Hudson, "Eating Disorders," *Textbook of Psychiatry/V,* 2nd Ed., p. 1862.

[2] Standard or traditional psychotherapy does not seem to greatly alter anorexic behavior, but behavioral therapy does seem to promise some hope.

[3] Pope and Hudson, "Eating Disorders," p. 1863.

[4] Pope and Hudson, "Eating Disorders," *Textbook of Psychiatry/V*, 5th ed., Vol. 2, pp. 1854–1864.

[5] Pope and Hudson, "Eating Disorders," p. 1858.

[6] Pope and Hudson, p. 1863.

[7] Pope and Hudson, p. 1863.

[8] Pope and Hudson, p. 1863.

[9] Pope and Hudson, p. 1863.

Resources for Help

American Anorexia/Bulimia Association, Inc. (AABA)
420 East 76th Street
New York, NY 10021
(212) 734-1114
(Phone lines manned 9 A.M. to 5 P.M. EST,
Monday through Friday)

National Association of Anorexia Nervosa and
Associated Disorders (ANAD)
P.O. Box 7
Highland Park, IL 60035
(708) 831-3438

Overeaters Anonymous Headquarters
World Services Office
383 Van Ness Avenue, Suite 1601
Torrance, CA 90501
(310) 618-8835

Suggested Readings

Bennett, William and Gurin, Joel, *The Dieter's Dilemma*, New York: Basic Books, 1982.

Boskind-White, M. and White, W. C., Jr., *Bulimarexia. The Binge/Purge Cycle*, London and New York: W. W. Norton and Company, 1983.

Bruch, Hilde, *Eating Disorders: Obesity, Anorexia, and the Person Within*, New York: Basic Books, 1973.

Bruch, Hilde, *The Golden Cage: The Enigma of Anorexia Nervosa*, Cambridge: Harvard University Press, 1978.

Brumberg, Joan J., *Fasting Girls: The History of Anorexia Nervosa*, Cambridge: Harvard University Press, 1988. Also by Penguin Books, New York, 1989.

Cauwels, Janice, *Bulimia: The Binge Purge Compulsion*, Garden City, N.Y.: Doubleday, 1983.

Chernin, Kim, *The Obsession: Reflections on the Tyranny of Slenderness*, New York: Harper & Row, 1981.

Chernin, Kim, *The Hungry Self: Women, Eating, and Identity*, New York: Harper & Row, 1985.

Crisp, Arthur, *Anorexia Nervosa: Let Me Be*, New York: Grune and Stratton, 1980.

Czyzewski, Danita and Suhr, Melanie, eds., *Hilde Bruch Conversations with Anorexics*, New York: Basic Books, Inc., 1988.

Dowling, Colette, *The Cinderella Complex*, Summit Books, 1981.

Friday, Nancy, *My Mother, Myself: The Daughter's Search for Identity*, New York: Dell, 1977.

Garfinkel, Paul and Garner, David, *Anorexia Nervosa: A Multidimensional Perspective*, New York: Brunner/Mazel, 1982.

Garner, David and Garfinkel, Paul, *Handbook of Psychotherapy for Anorexia Nervosa and Bulimia*, New York: Guilford Press, 1985.

Garner, David and Garfinkel, Paul, *The Role of Drug Treatment for Eating Disorders*, New York: Brunner/Mazel, 1987.

Hall, Lindsey and Cohn, Leigh, *Eating Without Fear: A Guide to Understanding and Overcoming Bulimia*, New York: Bantam Books, 1990.

Hirschmann, Jane and Zaphiropoulos, Lela, *Are You Hungry?*, New York: New American Library, 1987.

Jablow, Martha M., *A Parents' Guide to Eating Disorders and Obesity*, New York: Bantam, Doubleday, Dell Publishing Group, Inc., 1992.

Johnson, Craig and Conners, Mary, *The Etiology and Treatment of Bulimia Nervosa: A Biopsychological Perspective*, New York: Basic Books, 1987.

Kinoy, Barbara, Miller, Estelle B., Atchley, John A., and the Book Committee of the American Anorexia/Bulimia Association, *When Will We Laugh Again?: Living and Dealing with Anorexia Nervosa and Bulimia*, New York: Columbia University Press, 1984.

Levenkron, Steven, *Treating and Overcoming Anorexia Nervosa*, New York: Scribner's, 1982.

Macleod, Sheila, *The Art of Starvation: A Story of Anorexia and Survival*, New York: Schocken Books, 1982.

Meehan, V., Wilkes, N. J., and Howard, H. L., *Applying New Attitudes and Directions*, Highland Park, Ill., 1984.

Minuchin, Salvatore, Rosman, Bernice, and Baker, Lester, *Psychosomatic Families: Anorexia Nervosa in Context*, Cambridge: Harvard University Press, 1978.

Munter, Carol and Hirschmann, Jane, *Overcoming Overeating*, Reading, Mass.: Addison-Wesley, 1988.

Neuman, Patricia and Halvorson, Patricia, *Anorexia Nervosa and Bulimia: A Handbook for Counselors and Therapists*, New York: Van Nostrand Reinhold, 1983.

Orbach, Susie, *Fat Is a Feminist Issue*, New York: Paddington Press, 1978. Also Berkley Medallion Books, 1978.

Orbach, Susie, *Hunger Strike*, New York: W. W. Norton and Company, 1986.

Palazzoli, Mara, *Self Starvation: From Individual to Family Therapy in the Treatment of Anorexia Nervosa*, London: Human Context Books, Chaucer, 1974.

Root, M.P., Fallon, P., and Friedrich, W. N., *Bulimia: A Systems Approach to Treatment*, New York and London: W. W. Norton and Company, 1986.

Roth, Geneen, *Feeding the Hungry Heart*, New York: Signet, 1983.

Roth, Geneen, *Breaking Free from Compulsive Eating*, New York: Signet, 1986.

Seigel, Michele, Brisman, Judith, and Weinshel, Margot, *Surviving and Eating Disorder: Strategies for Family and Friends*, New York: Harper & Row, 1988.

Sours, John A., *Starving to Death in a Sea of Objects: The Anorexia Nervosa Syndrome*, New York and London: Jason Aronson, 1980.

Vallette, Brett, *A Parent's Guide to Eating Disorders*, New York: Avon Books, 1990.

Wilson, C. P., Hogan, C. C., and Mintz, I., *The Fear of Being Fat: The Treatment of Anorexia and Bulimia*, New York: Jason Aronson, 1983.

Winnicott, D. W., *Playing and Reality*, New York: Basic Books, 1971.

Most of these books should be available through your local library or through regional and national interlibrary loan programs that operate across the country. Many of them are currently in print and available or at least orderable at your local bookstore. Even those of you who may live in very rural or remote areas without a large library or bookstore nearby need not fear you will come up empty-handed in your search for information. The very helpful staff at the national offices of AA/BA in New York recommended an invaluable source of reading information to me that I will now pass along to you. Gurze Books of Carlsbad, California, is a book-distribution company that has specialized in books on eating disorders and related issues since 1980. For a toll-free call, this company will send their Bookshelf Catalogue, which contains virtually every book on these subjects currently in print. In your quest to become informed, you will be able to order any of these books that you find intriguing and have them delivered to your doorstep. Their address is: Gurze Books, P.O. Box 2238, Carlsbad, CA 92018. Toll free number: (800) 756-7533. Direct Dial number: (619) 434-7533.

Also, on the subject of binge eating or compulsive overeating, the World Service Office of Overeaters Anonymous provides a listing of mainly pamphlets that they will gladly send you, along with the information about starting a local Overeaters Anonymous chapter in your community. There may be a charge for some of the printed material and the video material they distribute. You can write them at P.O. Box 92870, Los Angeles, CA 90009, or call them at (213) 618-8835, for more information.

Bibliography

Blundell, John E., "Appetite Disturbance and the Problems of Overweight," *Drugs,* Vol. 39, Suppl. 3, 1990, pp. 1–19.

Booth, D.A., "Mood- and Nutrient-Conditioned Appetites. Cultural and Physiological Bases for Eating Disorders," *Annals of the New York Academy of Sciences,* Vol. 575, 1989, pp. 122–133.

Brewerton, Timothy, et al., "Dysregulation of 5-HT Function in Bulimia Nervosa," *Annals of the New York Academy of Sciences,* Vol. 575, 1989, pp. 500–501.

Brumberg, Joan J., *Fasting Girls. The History of Anorexia Nervosa,* Cambridge: Harvard University Press, 1988.

Drewnowski, Adam, "Taste Responsiveness in Eating Disorders," *Annals of the New York Academy of Sciences,* Vol. 575, 1989, pp. 398–407.

Farley, Dixie, "Eating Disorders Require Medical Attention," *FDA Consumer,* Vol. 26, No. 2, March 1992, pp. 27–29.

Geracioti, Thomas D., Jr., et al., "Meal-Related Cholecystokinin Secretion in Eating and Affective Disorders," *Psychopharmacology Bulletin,* Vol. 25, No. 3, 1989, pp. 444–449.

Hall, L. and Cohn, L., *Eating Without Fear,* New York: Bantam Books, 1990.

Heobel, B.G., et al., "Microdialysis Studies of Brain Norepinephrine, Serotonin, and Dopamine Release During Ingestive Behavior," *Annals of the New York Academy of Sciences,* Vol. 575, 1989, pp. 171–186.

Kaplan, Harold I. and Sadock, Benjamin J., eds., *Comprehensive Textbook of Psychiatry/V,* Vols. 1 and 2., Ed. 5, 1989.

Kelly, John T., "Bulimia Nervosa," *Medical Tribune,* April 14, 1988, pp. 17–19.

L., Elizabeth, *Twelve Steps for Overeaters: An Interpretation of the Twelve Steps of Overeaters Anonymous,* New York: HarperCollins Publishers, 1988.

Lange Textbook Series, "Eating Disorders," *Current Concepts in Psychiatry,* 1991, pp. 740–749.

Laurence, Leslie, "Eat What You Love—Without Feeling Bad," *McCall's,* May 1992, p. 80.

Leibowitz, Sarah, "Hypothalamic Neuropeptide Y, Galanin, and Amines. Concepts of Coexistence in Relation to Feeding Behavior," *Annals of the New York Academy of Sciences,* Vol. 575, 1989, pp. 221–233.

Leibowitz, Sarah, "The Role of Serotonin in Eating Disorders," *Drugs,* Vol. 39, Suppl. 3, 1990, pp. 33–39.

Levine, Allen and Billington, Charles, "Opiods. Are They Regulators of Feeding?" *Annals of the New York Academy of Sciences,* Vol. 575, 1989, pp. 209–215.

Samanin, Rosario and Garattini, Silvio, "Serotonin and the Pharmacology of Eating Disorders," *Annals of the New York Academy of Sciences,* Vol. 575, 1989, pp. 194–203.

Siegel, Michele, Brisman, Judith, and Weinshel, Margot, *Surviving and Eating Disorder,* New York: Harper & Row, 1988.

Yates, Alayne, "Current Perspectives on the Eating Disorders: I. History, Psychological and Biological Aspects," *Journal of the American Academy of Child and Adolescent Psychiatry,* 1989, pp. 813–828.

Stressor Worksheet

STRESSOR: _____

_____

_____

_____

FEELINGS: _____

_____

_____

_____

RESPONSE: _____

_____

_____

_____

REALITY CHECK: _____

_____

_____

_____

PLAN OF ACTION: _____

_____

_____

_____

_____

Index

Adrenalin, 40
Alcoholics Anonymous, 111
Alcoholism, 17, 81
Amenorrhea, 136
American Anorexia/Bulimia
    Association, Inc. (AABA), 29,
    113, 176
American Dietetic Association, 38
Amytriptyline, 144
Anafranil, 144
Anger, responding to, 86
Anorexia mirabilis, 33
Anorexia nervosa/anorectics
    "addiction to" model and, 45
    criteria for diagnosing, 23
    development of, 20
    educational attainment and, 21
    ethnic differences and, 20
    example of, 18–19
    gender and, 20
    historical background of, 33–34
    insecurity and, 57
    nutritional goals, 159–62
    perfectionism and, 57
    physical signs of, 20, 21–22, 58–
    59
    preoccupation with weight and
        food, 57
    profile of, 20–23
    signs of, 57–59
    social classes and, 20
    sources of help, 28–29

views of anorectics, 21, 22–23
    withdrawal from family/friends, 58
Antidepressants, 143–45
Antiseizure medications, 145–46
Appetite stimulants, 143
Approaching loved one, under the
    guidance of therapist, 84–89
Arrhythmias, 140

Barium swallow, 141
Bathroom, frequent trips to the, 63
Behavioral therapy, 126
Binge-eating disorder, 25
    bulimia nervosa and, 61–62
Biological model, 39–40
Bio Syn, Inc., 162
Bloating, 59
Blood chemistries, 137–39
Blood tests, diagnostic, 139
Brumberg, Joan Jacobs, 44
Bulimarexia, 20
Bulimia nervosa/bulimics
    "addiction to" model and, 46–48
    appearance of purge-related
        medications, 62
    binge eating and, 61–62
    caches/hoards of food and, 62–63
    criteria for diagnosing, 17–18
    development of, 14–15
    ethnic differences and, 13–14
    example of, 11–12
    exercise and, 16, 61

Bulimia nervosa/bulimics (*continued*)
  financial problems and, 63
  frequent trips to the bathroom, 63
  gender and, 13
  impulsiveness of, 17, 60
  insecurity and, 60
  missing food and, 62
  nutritional goals, 162–65
  physical signs of, 15–16, 64–66
  preoccupation with weight and
      food, 60–61, 64
  profile of, 13–20
  signs of, 59–66
  social classes and, 15
  sources of help, 28–29
  views of bulimics, 17
  volatile emotions and, 60
  vomiting and, 63

Carbamazepine, 146
Carbohydrate intake
  anorectics and, 161
  bulimics and, 163–64
  compulsive overeaters and, 166–67
Cardiac evaluation, 140
Carpenter, Karen, 62
Cheeks, swelling in the, 64
Chem Panel, 137
Chlorimipramine, 144
Cholecystokinin (CCK), 163
Clinical psychologist, licensing of, 75
Cold intolerance, 59
Colonoscopy, 141
Complete blood count (CBC), 137
Compulsive overeating/compulsive
    overeaters
  avoidance of recreational activities
      and, 67–68
  criteria for diagnosing, 26
  diet hopping and, 66–67
  eating like a bird, but are
      overweight, 66
  example of, 24
  gender and, 26
  hypertension and, 69
  mood swings and, 68

  nutritional goals, 165–67
  other names for, 25
  physical signs of, 69
  profile of, 26–27
  signs of, 66–69
  social classes and, 26–27
  sources of help, 29–30
  views of compulsive overeaters, 27
  weight equated with success and
      failure, 68
  weight fluctuations and, 69
Computer tomography (CT), 141
Confused thinking
  anorexia nervosa and, 58
  bulimia nervosa and, 64–65
Controlling Eating Disorders, 148–49
Coping strategies, 118
  analyzing feelings, 119–20, 121
  developing plan of action, 121–22
  reality check, 120, 121
  responding to feelings, 120, 121
  stressors, 119, 121
Counselor. *See* Therapist
Covey, Stephen, 106, 116
Cycloheptadine, 143

Defense mechanisms
  denial, 82–83
  externalizing, 83–84
  minimizing, 83
  rationalizing, 82
Denial, 82–83
  responding to, 87–88
Dental evaluation, 141
Depakene, 146
Depression, 135
Desipramine, 144
Desperation, feelings of, 53–54
Desyrel, 144
Dexamethasone Suppression Test,
    139
d-fenfluramine, 146
*Diagnostic and Statistical Manual of
    Mental Disorders* (DSM-III-R), 17
Diagnostic Profile, 137
Diet for a Small Planet, 160–61

Diet hopping, 66–67
Dilantin, 145–46
Dizziness
 anorexia nervosa and, 58
 bulimia nervosa and, 64–65
Drug abuse, bulimia nervosa and, 17
Drug therapy
 antidepressants, 143–45
 antiseizure medications, 145–46
 appetite stimulants, 143
 new drugs, 146
 opiate antagonists, 145

Eades, Michael R., 166
Eating disorders
 behaviors not associated with, 48–50
 differences between strange habits and, 50–51
 endogenous opiates and, 42–44
 reasons for, 51–54
 when you should respond to, 69–71
Eating disorders, signs of
 anorexia nervosa and, 56–59
 bulimia nervosa and, 59–66
 compulsive overeating and, 66–69
Eating disorders, theories of
 biological, 39–40
 combining the models, 44–48
 psychodynamic, 35–37
 sociocultural, 37–39
EGD, 141
Elavil, 144
Electrocardiogram (EKG), 140
Electroencephalograms (EEGs), 145
Emergencies, 78, 79
Emotions
 blunting of, 51
 bulimia nervosa and volatile, 60
 compulsive overeating and mood swings, 68
Endogenous opiates, 42–44
Endorphins, 42–43
Enkephalins, 42–43
Epinephrine, 40

Equilibrium, returning to, 105–7
Ethnic differences
 anorexia nervosa and, 20
 bulimia nervosa and, 13–14
Exercise, bulimics and, 16, 61
Exposure cue and response prevention, 126
Externalizing, 83–84
Eyes, puffy, 64

Fainting
 bulimia nervosa and, 64–65
 compulsive overeating and, 69
 responding to, 70–71
Family. See also Home environment
 continuing to heal the, 108–9
 counseling, 77
 dysfunction, 80–81
 history of other disorders, 135–36
 inventory of behaviors that can contribute to disorder, 79–81
 therapy, 128–32
Fasting Girls: The History of Anorexia Nervosa (Brumberg), 44
Fatigue, 64
Fat intake, anorectics and, 161–62
Feeding center, 39
Feelings
 analyzing, 119–120, 121
 responding to, 120, 121
Fiber, bulimics and, 164–65
Financial problems for bulimics, 63
Fluoxetine, 144
Follicle-stimulating hormone (FSH), 138–39
Food
 arrangement, 49
 caches/hoards of, 62–63
 issues, dealing with, 156–59
 missing, 62
Food, preoccupation with
 anorexia nervosa and, 57
 bulimia nervosa and, 60–61

Gastrocolic reflex, 63
Gastrointestinal evaluation, 140–41

Gender
  anorexia nervosa and, 20
  bulimia nervosa and, 13
  compulsive overeating and, 26
Genetics, relationship to eating
    disorders, 135–36
GI examination, upper, 141
Glasser, Michael, 106
Goals for progress, setting, 99–105
Group therapy, 126–28
Gut peptides, 163
Gynecologic evaluation, 136
Gynecologic history, 136

Health history, 132–35
Help, resources for, 28–30, 176
Help for loved one, steps for
    obtaining
  approaching loved one, under the
    guidance of therapist, 84–89
  become informed, 73–74
  contacting a therapist, 74–79
  continuing to heal the family,
    108–9
  family inventory of behaviors that
    contribute to disorder, 79–81
  formal intervention, 89–99
  preparing for resistance, 81–84
  recognizing your limits, 107
  returning to equilibrium, 105–7
  setting goals, 99–105
Help for yourself, steps for obtaining
  being committed in obtaining
    help, 113–14
  belief in a stronger power, 111–
    12
  coping strategies, 118–22
  help of others, 116–17
  making amends, 114–15
  recognizing addiction, 111, 113
  recognizing need for help, 114
  self-examination inventory, 112–
    13, 115–16
  sharing recovery with others, 117–
    18
Holter monitor, 140

Home environment. *See also* Family
  creating a healthier, 150–51
  importance of letting go, 151–52
  rebuilding relationships, 152–54
  respecting her rights, 154–56
Hospitalization, 147–48
How to Lower Your Fat Thermostat
    (Remington, Fisher and Parent),
    166
Human Genome Project, 135–36
Hypertension, 69
Hypothalamus, 39

Imipramine, 144
Imitrex, 146
Impulsive behavior, bulimics and, 17,
    60
Indignation, responding to, 86–87
Individual therapy, 125–26
Insecurity
  anorexia nervosa and, 57
  bulimia nervosa and, 60
Insulin, serum, 138
Insurance coverage, 77–78
Intervention steps/dialogue, 89–99
Ipecac syrup, 62, 140
Isocarboxazide, 144

Jacobs, Sarah, 34

Kleptomania, 60
Konsyl, 165

Laboratory evaluation
  blood chemistries, 137–39
  diagnostic blood tests, 139
  toxicology, 140
Lanugo, 59
Lean body weight, determining, 166
Leverage, use of, 92–93
Licensed social worker (LCSW), 75–76
Luteinizing hormone (LH), 138–39

Magnetic resonance imaging (MRI),
    141
Maintenance. *See* Relapse

Marplan, 144
Medical evaluation
    family history, 135–36
    gynecologic evaluation, 136
    gynecologic history, 136
    health history, 132–35
Menstrual irregularities, 59, 136
Metamucil, 165
Minimizing, 83
Monoamine oxidase inhibitors, 144
Mood elevation, 52–53
Mood swings, compulsive overeating
    and, 68
Muscle aches and cramping, 64

Nalaxone, 43, 143
Narcan, 145
Narcotics Anonymous, 111
Nardil, 144
National American Association for
    the Study of Obesity, 146
National Association of Anorexia
    Nervosa and Associated
    Disorders (ANAD), 29, 113, 176
Neuropeptide Y (NPY), 42
Neuroreceptors, 39
Neurotransmitters
    neuropeptide Y, 42
    norepinephrine, 40–41
    role of, 39
    serotonin, 41, 52
Night-eaters syndrome, 25
Norepinephrine (NE), 40–41, 139
Norpramin, 144
Nuclei, 39
Nutritional evaluation and
    reeducation, 142–43
Nutritional goals
    anorexia nervosa and, 159–62
    bulimia nervosa and, 162–65
    compulsive overeating and, 165–67

Obese bulimia, 25
Omega Syn, 162
Opiate antagonists, 145
Opinions, right to one's, 154

Oryx Publishing Co., 149
Overeaters Anonymous, 29–30, 111,
    176

Pain, blunting of, 51
Pallor, 59
Parnate, 144
Parotid gland, 64
Perfectionism, 57
Periactin, 143
Phenytoin, 145–46
Physical signs
    of anorexia nervosa, 20, 21–22,
        58–59
    of bulimia nervosa, 15–16, 64–66
    of compulsive overeating, 69
Plan of action, developing, 121–22
Privacy, right of, 155
Proctosigmoidoscopy, 141
Projection, responding to, 87
Protein intake
    anorectics and, 160–61
    bulimics and, 163
    compulsive overeaters and, 165–66
Prozac, 144–45
Psychiatrist, licensing of, 75
Psychodynamic model, 35–37
Psychosomatic complaints, 59
Psychotherapy
    family, 128–32
    group, 126–28
    individual, 125–26
    role of, 124–25
Purge-related medications, 62

QT interval, prolonged, 140

Rationalizing, 82
Reality check, 120, 121
Recovery. See Help; Therapies
Recreational activities, avoidance of,
    67–68
Relapse
    awareness, 167–68
    handling, 170–71
    spotting, 168–70

Relationships, rebuilding, 152–54
Relief, responding to, 88–89
Reproductive hormones, 138–39
Resistance, preparing for, 81–84
    hospitalization and, 147–48
Rights, respecting, 154–56

Satiety center, 39
Self, validating of, 53
Self-examination, 79–81
    inventory, 112–13, 115–16
Serenity Prayer, 107
Serotonin (5HT), 41, 52, 139
Serotonin reuptake inhibitors, 144
Sertraline, 144
Serum insulin, 138
Serum norepinephrine and serotonin
    (5HT), 139
7 Habits of Highly Effective People
    (Covey), 106, 116
Sexual problems, bulimics and, 17
SMAC, 137
SMA-24, 137
Social classes
    anorexia nervosa and, 20
    bulimia nervosa and, 15
    compulsive overeating and, 26–27
Social withdrawal, 58, 71
Sociocultural model, 37–39
Sore throat, chronic, 65–66
Spike, 40
Spitzer, Robert L., 25
Stomachache, 59
Stressors, 119, 121, 182–83
Suicidal talk/gestures, 70
Sumatriptan, 146

Take Effective Control of Your Life
    (Glasser), 106
Tegretol, 146
Therapies
    cardiac evaluation, 140
    dental evaluation, 141
    drug therapy, 143–46
    gastrointestinal evaluation, 140–
    41

laboratory evaluation, 137–40
medical evaluation, 132–36
nutritional evaluation and
    reeducation, 142–43
psychotherapy, 124–32
Therapist
    approaching loved one, under the
        guidance of, 84–89
    approach taken by, 76–77
    asking for credentials, 76
    contacting a, 74–79
    family counseling and, 77
    licensing of, 75–76
    questions to ask at the first
        meeting, 77–79
    your goals with a, 31–32
Thin So Fast (Eades), 166
Thyroid-stimulating hormone
    (TSH), 138
Thyroid studies, 137–38
Thyrotropin-releasing hormone
    (TRH), 138
Tofranil, 144
Tooth decay, 65, 141
Toxicology, 140
Trazadone lithium carbonate, 144
Treatment facilities, 148–49
Twelve Step Recovery. See Help for
    yourself, steps for obtaining

Valproic acid, 146
Vitamins
    anorectics and, 162
    bulimics and, 164
Void, filling the, 52
Vomiting, 63

Weight, determining lean body, 166
Weight, preoccupation with
    anorexia nervosa and, 57, 58
    bulimia nervosa and, 60–61, 64
Weight problems, compulsive
    overeating and, 66–67, 68, 69
Withdrawal symptoms, 58, 71

Zoloft, 144

About the Author

Mary Dan Eades was born and raised in Hot Springs, Arkansas. She graduated magna cum laude from the University of Arkansas, and in 1981 she received her M.D. from the university's School of Medical Science. In 1982, she and her husband, Michael Eades, M.D., opened the first of a chain of out-patient clinics in Little Rock, Arkansas, specializing in family medicine. After ten years in general and family practice, she has recently joined her husband in a practice devoted solely to the care of weight-related diseases. She is a member of the American Society of Bariatric Physicians and an associate member of the North American Association for the Study of Obesity. She is also the author of *If It Runs in Your Family: Breast Cancer* and *If It Runs in Your Family: Arthritis*. Dr. Eades makes her home in Little Rock with her husband and three sons.